Handpicked Italy

A MR. & MRS. ITALY GUIDE

MAX PUBLICATIONS, INC.

825 Malvern Hill | Alpharetta, Georgia 30022 | USA: ++770-851-0935

E-mail: info@mrandmrsitaly.com | Website: www.mrandmrsitaly.com

Dedication

To Italy's earthquake families, rescuers and survivors, particularly those hardest hit villages of Amatrice, Pescara del Tronto and Accumoli.

Acknowledgments

To our sons, Ari, Isaac, and Jacob, and to Jacobs's wife, Nora, and their children Kai and Ili. You are the wind beneath our wings!

Photo Credits

Front Cover – Top left: Under the superb artistic talent of Chef Fabio Iacovone, the culinary program at Bellevue Hotel & Spa in Cogne offers guests a variety of eateries featuring regional and international cuisine, including the *Michelin* one-star Bellevue. Top right: Sleep in a medieval tower-turned-suite at Hotel Brunelleschi Firenze, located on the top of the property's magnificent Pagliazza Tower. The suite overlooks some of the highlights of the city of Florence, including Giotto's bell tower, Brunelleschi's dome, the Ghiberti tower, and the Palazzo Vecchio. Bottom left: Punta Tragara offers guests access to the beauty for which the island of Capri is famous, but in a secluded setting far away from the summer crowds. Bottom right: Every window in the individual rooms and suites of Castel Monastero in Siena opens onto a charming series of bucolic vistas, from sweeping vineyards to lush woods to the verdant fields of Castelnuovo Berardenga.

Opposite – Therasia Resort Sea & Spa is located on the island of Vulcano, the southernmost of the seven Aeolian Islands that comprise a volcanic archipelago in the Tyrrhenian Sea north of Sicily

Table of Contents – Lefay Resort & SPA Lago di Garda, the first Lake Garda property to be awarded the prestigious five-star superior rating, is located in the heart of the spectacular Riviera dei Limoni. It is surrounded by lush woods, gentle rolling hills, and natural terraces rich in olive trees.

Page 6 & 7 – At Sicily's Verdura Resort all suites have sea views, and seamlessly meld indoor and outdoor spaces. Two ambassador and one presidential suite pictured feature separate living, kitchen, dining, and sleeping areas, as well as interior courtyards and outdoor terraces that open to expansive views.

Contributors: Claudia Camerino is a social media specialist who has been instrumental in assisting Mr. & Mrs. Italy with developing, coordinating, and executing social media strategies across a variety of platforms, as well as curating and articulating a brand persona. Based in Portland, Oregon, but with family in Venice, Italy, Claudia has been privileged to explore the stunning natural beauty and unmatched culinary culture of Italy. A natural trend spotter, she has a passion for making the foreign familiar and the familiar foreign.

Rena Distasio has sixteen years of freelance writing, editing, and researching experience. She specializes in helping authors polish their book-length manuscripts for submission and publication, and writes on a number of subjects for various magazines and websites. She also serves as an editor for *Trend* magazine, a bi-annual publication covering Southwestern art, architecture, and design for a global readership. She has worked as a writer and editor for Mr. & Mrs. Italy Guides since 2008.

Caleb Hopkins is a certified sommelier with the Court of Master Sommeliers. With over a decade of experience in beverage management throughout the United States, including Hawaii, he regularly competes in sommelier competitions, has served as a wine judge for the Pacific Northwest Wine competition in Oregon, and travels extensively to immerse himself in the wine culture of Europe, with Italy being one of his favorite spots.

Book Designer: With nearly twenty-five years of creating and producing books, Jill Dible has lent her talents to such publishers as Longstreet Press, Vineyard Stories, Dalmation Press, and the Bookhouse Group. She has also worked on publications for the Federal Reserve Bank of Atlanta, the American Cancer Society, the Arthritis Foundation, Habitat for Humanity, and Atlanta's Piedmont Hospital. She also designs yearly collector's edition publications on the University of Georgia Bulldogs, the Clemson Tigers, and the Alabama Crimson Tide football teams.

Publishing Software: This print and digital book was created by Ken Jones of Circular Software. Ken, a publishing software expert with over ten years of experience in technical production management, software training, and software development (most recently at DK and Penguin Group UK), now specializes in writing workflow applications and in training and consultancy for publishers on print and digital workflows. He founded Circular Software to provide software tools and services for a range of illustrated book publishing customers, and his clients include Hachette Book Group, Macmillan Publishers, Penguin Random House, and Thames & Hudson. For this publication, Ken used Circular Software's unique tools to run production checks with GreenLight, share a live flatplan and receive comments with MasterPlan, and generate the EPUB and online searchable eBook using CircularFLO. For more information, log onto circularsoftware.com.

Contents

INTRODUCTION

One of the great joys of traveling through Italy is discovering firsthand that it is, indeed, a dream destination. Its countryside has long enticed visitors with its timeless beauty, from romantic, undulating plains to majestic Alpine peaks to miles of uninterrupted white beaches. Its cities are both repositories for some of the world's greatest art and architecture, as well as bustling centers of fashion and industry. Likewise, three millennia of traditions have formed distinctive personalities among the Italians themselves, who continue to charm visitors from across the globe with their hospitality and warmth.

Italy is also famous as one of the world's top epicurean destinations. Whether you seek authentic culinary experiences or modern reinterpretations of classic dishes, your options are endless. As are your opportunities to indulge in exceptional regional wines.

Most travelers believe that the best food and drink in Italy is to be found in its restaurants, whether rustic *trattorias*, family-run *osterias*, or elegant Michelin-stared *ristorantes*. Rarely do foodies consider their hotels. Outside of a quick cup of coffee and a pastry in the mornings, most culinary adventurers seek their sustenance elsewhere, adhering to the maxim that hotel food is usually mediocre food.

Mr. & Mrs. Italy has discovered the exceptions to that rule.

After years of staying in some of Italy's finest hotels and resorts, Mr. & Mrs. Italy realized that many of these venues not only offer exceptional luxury accommodations they also support outstanding culinary programs. The owners of these properties know that food is important to the discriminating traveler and they have developed on-site restaurants with exceptional ambiance, passionate and talented chefs, and wine lists that reflect the best local and regional offerings.

A Luxury Travel Experience

While there are plenty of magazines and books that cater to singles, couples, and budget travelers, few take into consideration the needs of travelers seeking luxury accommodations and authentic, immersive experiences—including culinary experiences—in Italy's foremost destination cities.

The Mr. & Mrs. Italy Guides and website fill this void by offering a host of luxury accommodations that exemplify the romance for which Italy is famous. Whatever your plans, these are places where you can indulge your senses and truly celebrate la dolce vita.

Exceptional Accommodations

Mr. & Mrs. Italy presents a specially selected group of leading hotels, resorts, villas, historic houses, and castles located in

ABOVE: On the Italian Riviera of Flowers, just south of the chic resort town of Monte Carlo, enjoy breakfast on the terrace of Royal Hotel Sanremo; the deluxe penthouse suites in particular offer stunning vistas over the sea.

OPPOSITE: Castello di Tornano is set amid the gently rolling hills of Gaiole in Chianti. Dotted with vineyards and olive groves, the hamlet offers visitors an unparalleled Tuscan experience.

Italy's most preferred destinations. These properties are distinguished by their management's passion for providing unique luxury hospitality experiences, along with the best food and wine to be found in the region. Many are renowned for award-winning or five-star service and amenities. Others have earned distinction for unique features—outstanding views, privileged locations, Gambero Rosso or Michelin star rated cuisine, extensive wine lists, one-of-a-kind antiques, alluring architecture and décor, historical significance, beautiful natural surroundings, and secluded beaches.

Most importantly, each property meets Mr. & Mrs. Italy's highest standards for luxury travel.

About the Publisher

Mr. & Mrs. Italy is a dynamic family-run company representing an extraordinary group of select hotels and resorts offering unsurpassed services to an elite clientele. Our first guidebook, *Italy's Best with Kids*, was a self-publishing phenomenon, transcending a humble beginning to end up a brisk seller in major chain bookstores. Our second book, *Italy Luxury Family Hotels and Resorts*, enjoyed a three-edition run, and is still considered one of the must-have publications for luxury travel.

With years of experience exploring every region of Italy, Mr. & Mrs. Italy has visited, slept in, inspected, eaten at, and developed close personal relationships with the owners and management of all our choice properties. In our quest to seek out the best Italy has to offer, we have skied the Italian Alps, toured the art centers of Rome, Florence, and Venice, inspected hotel kitchens and assisted with food preparation, sailed the archipelago islands, scuba dived in the Mediterranean, and luxuriated on some of the country's most exclusive beaches.

Because of our relationships with our recommended properties, visitors to Italy often comment that as soon as they identify themselves as a Mr. & Mrs. Italy Traveler, they are greeted with extra warm recognition. Time and again these travelers go on to report special VIP treatments upon arrival, ranging from little extras like early check-ins and late checkouts, to room upgrades and welcome gifts in their rooms. These are just a few of the many perks extended to our Mr. & Mrs. Italy Travelers.

Join Us!

The Mr. & Mrs. Italy Guides reveal select leading hotels, resorts, villas, and castles throughout Italy, for travelers of all ages who desire unique and immersive experiences. Whether you seek travel planning recommendations for the ideal places to sleep and eat while immersed in this outstandingly beautiful country or you would like to become part of the brand as one of our approved Mr. & Mrs. Italy Luxury Hotels, Mr. & Mrs. Italy Partners, or Mr. & Mrs. Italy Travel Specialists, we invite you to join our team. Call ++770-851-0935, or log onto www.mrandmrsitaly.com to learn more about how you can benefit from our expert knowledge of this endearing country.

Using this Guide

This Mr. & Mrs. Italy Guide is divided into three sections—Northern, Central, and Southern Italy—each with their corresponding geographical regions, the distinguishing features of those regions, and their individual luxury properties.

Each review provides information on that property's history, its services, amenities, and bars and restaurants, along with suggestions on things to do and see in the surrounding areas. The Fine Points at the end of each review provide a quick summary of property highlights, including what we enjoyed most about our stay, with a focus on culinary highlights.

WHAT SETS US APART

Mr. & Mrs. Italy's handpicked accommodations are more than just places to stay!

Mr. & Mrs. Italy believe that the greatest joy of travel is discovering and experiencing new cultures. That is why their recommended accommodations are more than just places to stay. Whether located in the heart of Rome or in the rolling hills of the Tuscan countryside, their handpicked properties offer visitors the opportunity to engage firsthand with the people and traditions that make Italy so remarkable.

Part of that engagement involves enjoyment of Italy's rich culinary heritage, showcased in both authentic local fare as well as inventive fusions of local and international styles. From family-run chalets in the heart of the Alps to the most exclusive accommodations on the Mediterranean Sea, all Mr. & Mrs. Italy properties are notable for food and wine programs that will impress even the most discriminating and experienced travelers.

In a quest to seek out the best Italy has to offer, Mr. & Mrs. Italy have skied the Italian Alps; toured hotel kitchens and assisted with food preparation; sailed the archipelago islands; scuba dived in the Mediterranean; swam the waters of the Sea of Sardinia, Strait of Sicily, and the Adriatic, Ionian, Tyrrhenian, and Ligurian seas; luxuriated on their most exclusive beaches; and immersed themselves in the art centers of Rome, Florence, and Venice. Throughout the years exploring every region of Italy, they have visited, slept in, eaten at, and developed close personal relationships with the owners and management of a fabulous collection of Italy's choicest hotels, resorts, and boutique properties.

Through their full-service custom tour-planning business, they bring that extensive knowledge to travelers seeking the same immersive experiences. Whether this is your first trip or a return visit, Mr. & Mrs. Italy will work closely with you to tailor an adventure that meets your individual needs, interests, and travel style. Are you a wine lover? They'll arrange a private tasting at one of their favorite local vineyards. Outdoor enthusiast? They know the best spots to bike, ski, golf, and hike. Is five-star spa pampering more your style? They'll craft an itinerary that will leave you relaxed, rejuvenated, and inspired.

If an Italian vacation is your dream, contact Mr. & Mrs. Italy to make it a reality.

Making Your Way through Italy

Designing Your Itinerary

This chapter is designed to assist you with the advanced planning required to develop your ideal and personalized visit. To facilitate your seamless navigation through this diverse country, we have included three large-scale maps: one highlights Italy's major cities, provinces, roads, and water features; the second provides estimated travel times between the most popular destination cities; and the third lists all major Italian airports, where European-based carriers like the ones noted on www.edreams.com will easily connect you to all ports throughout the country. In addition, a second distance chart highlights in kilometers the most important point-to-point distances between major cities.

How to Use Maps & Charts

We recommend you begin your planning by reading our "Highlights of the Regions" section, which will provide you with a great overview of Italy, including major cities, surrounding attractions, and places to stay. Say, for instance, you decide to spend your summer holiday experiencing the exquisite beaches and sights in Sicily. For an overall perspective, view the main map of Italy, which highlights each region's major cities, provinces, roads, and water features. The areas in Sicily you may want to consider visiting are Palermo, Agrigento, and Taormina, with a worthwhile excursion to the Aeolian Island of Lipari. Next, view the estimated time and distance maps, and/or consult the major Italian airports map for the best ports. Most itineraries can be done in reverse, and in many instances you can fly into one port and out

of another. Then visit the websites of the hotels reviewed in this guidebook. If using the eBook version, just click on the live links, which bring you directly to the hotels' websites and emails.

Special Offer

Once you have booked room nights at a Mr. & Mrs. Italy hotel, forward your reservation confirmation to travel@mrandmrsitaly.com. We will contact the hotel on your behalf and inform them you are a Mr. & Mrs. Italy VIP traveler, which qualifies you for upgrades and other distinguished services, according to availability.

ABOVE: Drink wine, eat cheese, and explore the canals of Venice. Mr. & Mrs. Italy travelers Zack, Lara, Caitlin, and Wesley enjoy some local *ciccheti* (snacks) as they learn the traditional *voga alla veneta*, the rowing style made famous by Venetian goldoliers.

OPPOSITE: The Borgo Scopeto Relais. Surrounded by pristine countryside, this little corner of paradise overlooks the city of Siena and the surrounding Chianti hills, a great location from which to explore one of the world's great art cities.

ITALY'S MAJOR CITIES, PROVINCES, ROADS, AND WATER FEATURES

Valle d'Aosta
Aosta
Biella
Novara
Vercelli
Turin
Asti
Alessandria
Cuneo
Piedmonte

Verbania
Varese
Como
Lecco
Lago Maggiore
Sondrio
Lombardia
Bergamo
Brescia
Milan
Monza e Brianza
Lodi
Pavia
Piacenza
Cremona
Mantova
Lago di Como
Lago di Garda

Bolzano
Trentino-Alto Adige
Trento
Belluno
Friuli-Venezia Giulia
Udine
Pordenone
Gorizia
Trieste
Vicenza
Verona
Padova
Treviso
Veneto
Venice
Gulf of Venice
Rovigo

Parma
Reggio nell'Emilia
Modena
Ferrara
Bologna
Emilia-Romagna
Ravenna

Liguria
Genoa
Savona
Gulf of Genoa
La Spezia
Carrara
Massa
Pistoia
Lucca
Prato
Florence
Forlì
Cesena
Rimini
Pesaro

Imperia

Livorno
Pisa
Ligurian Sea
Tuscany
Arezzo
Siena
Isola di Capraia
Elba
Grosseto

Urbino
Ancona
Marche
Macerata
Fermo
Perugia
Lago Trasimeno
Umbria
Ascoli Piceno
Terni
Viterbo
Lago di Bolsena
Lazio
Rieti
Lago di Bracciano
Vatican City
Rome
Latina

Teramo
Pescara
L'aquila
Chieti
Abruzzi

Frosinone
Isernia
Molise
Campobasso
Foggia
Barletta
Trani
Bari
Adriatic Sea

Campania
Benevento
Caserta
Avellino
Andria
Naples
Salerno
Potenza
Matera
Puglia
Brindisi
Taranto
Lecce
Basilicata
Gulf of Taranto

Sassari
Olbia
Tempio
Pausania
Nuoro
Sardinia
Ogliastra
Oristano
Medio Campidano
Iglesias
Cagliari
Carbonia

Tyrrhenian Sea

Calabria
Cosenza
Crotone
Catanzaro
Ionian Sea
Vibo Valentia

Mediterranean Sea

Isole Eolie [Aeolian Islands]
Lipari
Messina
Reggio di Calabria

Trapani
Palermo
Sicily
Enna
Catania
Agrigento
Caltanissetta
Siracusa
Ragusa
Strait of Sicily
Isola di Pantelleria
Malta Channel
Mediterranean Sea

ESTIMATED
DRIVING TIMES

ITALY

Sardinia

Sicily

Cogne — Stresa 2.5 hrs — Como
Stresa 1.25 hr Como
Cogne 1.75 hrs Turin
Stresa 1.75 hrs Turin
Como 1 hr Milan
Bolzano 1.75 hrs Cortina
Cortina 2.75 hrs Udine
Bolzano 1.5 hrs Verona
Bolzano 3 hrs Bologna
Cortina 2 hrs Venice
Udine 1 hr Venice
Milan 2 hrs Verona
Verona 1.75 hrs Venice
Verona 1.5 hrs Bologna
Venice 2 hrs Bologna
Milan 2 hrs Turin
Milan 2.25 hrs Bologna
Milan 2 hrs Genoa
Turin 2 hrs Genoa
Turin 2.75 hrs Genoa
Turin 2 hrs San Remo
Genoa 5 hr Portofino
Genoa 3 hrs Bologna
Portofino 1.5 hrs San Remo
Nice 5 hrs San Remo
Genoa 2 hrs Florence
Portofino 1.75 hrs Pisa
Portofino 2 hrs Florence
Bologna 1.5 hrs Florence
Bologna 1.5 hrs Pesaro
Pisa 1.25 hrs Florence
Florence 1 hr Siena
Florence 3.5 hrs Pesaro
Siena 2 hrs Perugia
Pesaro 2.25 hrs Pescara
Pisa 1.75 hrs Siena
Pisa 1.75 hrs Grosseto
Siena 1.25 hrs Grosseto
Siena 1.5 hrs Perugia
Grosseto 2.75 hrs Rome
Grosseto 2.5 hrs Rome
Siena 2.25 hrs Rome
Perugia 3 hrs Pescara
Pescara 2 hrs Campobasso
Campobasso 3 hrs Bari
Pescara 3 hrs Bari
Rome 2 hrs Naples
Naples 3.25 hrs Campobasso
Campobasso 2 hrs Naples
Naples 2 hrs Salerno
Naples 1 hr Salerno
Salerno 1.25 hrs Potenza
Naples 2 hrs Potenza
Potenza 2 hrs Bari
Bari 2 hrs Lecce
Naples 3.25 hrs Cosenza
Potenza 3 hrs Cosenza
Cosenza 2 hrs Villa San Giovani
Alghero 2 hrs Olbia
Alghero 2.5 hrs Guspini
Olbia 3.5 hrs Cagliari
Guspini 1 hr Cagliari
Messina Ferry 5 hr Aeolian Islands
Messina .75 hrs Villa San Giovani
Palermo .75 hrs Cefalu
Palermo 1.75 hrs Marsala
Cefalu 2.25 hrs Taormina
Cefalu 1.75 hrs Messina
Marsala 2 hrs Agrigento
Marsala 2.25 hrs Agrigento
Taormina 1 hr Catania
Agrigento 1 hr Falconara
Catania 2 hrs Agrigento
Catania 1.75 hrs Ragusa
Falconara 1.5 hrs Ragusa

MAJOR ITALIAN
AIRPORT LOCATIONS

DRIVING DISTANCES
Kilometers between main locations:

	Bari	Bologna	Bolzano	Florence	Genoa	Milan	Naples	Palermo	Rome	Turin	Trieste	Venice
Agrigento	703	1314	1571	1202	1437	1504	748	127	958	1600	1599	1460
Ancona	464	226	507	352	529	441	394	1142	306	559	517	378
Aosta	1067	405	456	477	248	186	947	1642	759	114	589	450
Arezzo	645	188	444	75	314	376	416	1109	228	472	473	334
Assisi	548	250	531	173	407	465	385	1079	197	571	484	344
Bari	—	670	948	702	937	882	262	667	432	1000	958	819
Bologna	670	—	287	131	309	221	587	1281	398	339	295	155
Bolzano	948	287	—	386	411	288	842	1537	654	411	365	226
Catania	542	1153	1410	1041	1276	1343	587	210	797	1439	1438	1314
Como	935	273	321	371	191	51	828	1522	639	168	454	316
Cortina	899	291	133	411	540	417	867	1561	678	540	247	160
Florence	702	131	386	—	251	318	473	1168	285	414	413	274
Genoa	882	309	411	251	—	142	712	1407	524	170	537	398
Lucca	776	163	419	77	164	280	547	1241	358	328	448	308
Milan	882	221	288	318	142	—	774	1468	585	142	416	276
Naples	262	587	842	473	712	774	—	714	229	872	871	732
Palermo	667	1281	1537	1168	1407	1468	714	—	922	1564	1563	1424
Parma	766	105	282	203	207	125	660	1352	472	244	388	249
Perugia	566	237	520	151	386	453	372	1066	183	549	470	331
Piacenza	820	159	271	257	152	68	714	1408	525	183	404	265
Pisa	807	194	451	108	170	286	578	1273	334	334	479	340
Reggio Calabria	453	1064	1321	953	1187	1254	499	241	708	1351	1350	1211
Rimini	560	117	398	243	420	331	515	1238	375	450	408	268
Roma	432	398	654	285	524	585	229	922	—	684	683	543
Salerno	242	627	884	515	750	817	56	662	271	913	912	773
Sanremo	1076	430	532	377	148	271	847	1541	659	233	665	526
Siena	660	177	433	75	299	367	431	1125	243	463	462	326
Taormina	496	1107	1364	995	1230	1297	541	261	751	1393	1392	1253
Turin	1000	339	411	414	170	142	872	1564	684	—	545	405
Venice	819	155	226	274	398	276	732	1424	543	405	163	—
Verona	815	153	154	252	295	172	708	1402	519	295	257	118

Sardinia

	Nuoro	Olbia	Oristano	Sassari
Cagliari	181	274	98	215
Nuoro		104	89	120
Olbia			83	103
Oristano				123
Sassari				

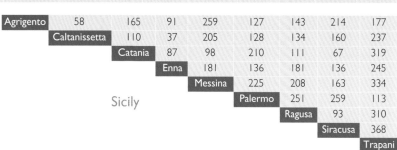

Sicily

	Caltanissetta	Catania	Enna	Messina	Palermo	Ragusa	Siracusa	Trapani
Agrigento	58	165	91	259	127	143	214	177
Caltanissetta		110	37	205	128	134	160	237
Catania			87	98	210	111	67	319
Enna				181	136	181	136	245
Messina					225	208	163	334
Palermo						251	259	113
Ragusa							93	310
Siracusa								368
Trapani								

The Fine Art of Italian Wine

There has never been a better time to enjoy Italian wine. Whether you are a wine connoisseur, or just want to drink a glass of good vino every now and then, Italy offers something for every palate.

If you have ever visited Italy, you know that it is covered in vineyards. They span from just below the Alps down to the heel of the boot and on to the islands of Sicily and Sardinia. Italy is home to twenty major wine-growing regions, each of which has its own culture and produces its own unique style of wine.

The French concept of *terroir* easily applies to Italy. Simply translated, *terroir* means "a sense of place." In winemaking, *terroir* encompasses everything that interacts with the grape and makes it unique to its region—soil type, climate, and geography, to name just several factors. Every time you drink a wine from a specific region not only are you are immediately transported there but you are also drinking a vintage that is truly unique. A great *terroir*-driven Barolo, a red wine made from the Nebbiolo grape in Piedmont, will never taste like a Nebbiolo grown elsewhere. Sommeliers only blind taste classic wines that show their *terrior*. It's no parlor trick; it takes years of practice to identify a wine without looking at its label, to learn which characteristics define taste as well as region. Like other great winegrowing

regions, Italy offers visitors the opportunity to sample wines that show a great sense of place.

If you've traveled to Italy, you are likely familiar with the scope of its landscape. From the flowing hillsides of classic medieval Tuscan villages like Cortona to the breathtaking cliff-side vineyards of the Cinque Terre, Italy's terrain, wine, and culture are as varied as they are beautiful. Until recent history, Italy was not a cohesive country so much as it was a collection of small self-governing regions. This is reflected in its culture and mirrored in its individual wines. For example, Trentino-Alto Adige, annexed by Italy in 1919, lists both German, and Italian as its official languages. Many of its winemaking techniques and laws differ from regions located farther south.

As such, learning about Italy's wine culture can quickly become overwhelming. So rather than inundate you with a barrage of facts about the sub-regions of Chianti, or subtle nuances of every soil type, we will focus instead on the top wines of each region and suggest some basic food pairings.

Visiting Wineries

The best way to begin your understanding of Italian winemaking culture is to experience it firsthand. Every winemaker I have encountered in Italy has been hospitable and happy to teach me about his or her particular style. Whenever

ABOVE: The cellar of Villa La Massa, situated in the mill beneath Il Verrocchio restaurant, exudes the charm and atmosphere of an old Tuscan wine cellar and is the ideal place for private tasting parties.

OPPOSITE: At the only five-star hotel in the heart of Siena, the Grand Hotel Continental, indulge in some of Italy's most important vintages from the on-site wine cellar, which is carved into the base of the medieval tower.

possible, I suggest visiting the wineries, taking any tours that are available, participating in tastings, and asking questions. Just remember, appointments are usually necessary. If you can't visit a winery, explore your hotel's offerings. Many of the properties featured in this book, for instance, have superb cellars that heavily focus on regional wines as well as vintages that you may be unable to find elsewhere. Most cities have *enotecas* as well. These are wine shops that typically offer tastings of wine from all over the region.

Italian Wine Classifications

In order to understand the dichotomy of Italian wines, you need a basic knowledge of the Italian wine classification system. Created in 1963, the Denominazione di Origine Controllata (DOC), is similar in design to the French AOC system in that it stipulates a geographical boundary and establishes how much and what types of grapes may be grown. It also covers certain viticulture techniques, alcohol levels, and aging requirements.

The Denominazione di Origine Controllata e Garantita (DOCG) is an even higher level of quality. It was created in 1963 as well, but the first DOCG designations were not awarded until 1980. Brunello di Montalcino, Barolo, and Vino Nobile di Montepulciano were the first DOCs to receive the prestigious DOCG honor.

Unfortunately, a wine stating DOCG is not an automatic guarantee of quality. The system has been regularly criticized for not being strict enough and for allowing huge expansions of already existing boundaries. Shortly after its inception, many of the winemakers became disillusioned with the DOCG. In Tuscany in 1968, Marchese Mario Incisa della Rocchetta released Sassicaia, in an effort to realize his dream of creating a Bordeaux-style blend. It was mostly Cabernet Sauvignon, with a little Cabernet Franc. Because it did not fall into the DOC-allowed grape varieties, however, it was classified as a *vino da tavola,* or table wine. The Marchese's blend also ushered in similar attempts, which in the process established a new wave of ultra-premium wines that have become known as the "Super Tuscans." While these wines have no legal meaning, they typically stipulate a red wine from Tuscany that utilizes non-indigenous grapes. Ornellaia, Tignanello, and countless other iconic Italian wines had their start in this so-called lowest category of Italian wine.

In 1992 the Government passed Goria's Law, which created a new category of wine classification called Indicazione Geografica Tipica (IGT). This category is a stepping stone for DOC. Once DOC, areas may apply for DOCG after five years and many are labeled by variety, which refers to a grape. For example, Sangiovese, the most-planted grape in Tuscany.

Grapes

It is said that there are over one thousand native grape varieties grown in Italy. This guide will focus on the major grapes that make the finest wines. It is important to remember that most Italian wines are blends of multiple grapes. So unlike in the United States, Italian wine labels generally indicate the location in which the wine's grapes were grown, rather than the specific grape itself. However, many wines that fall into the IGT category are now beginning to list grape varieties. This has been a boon for international sales, since the sometimes-confusing Italian wine labeling system could deter the average buyer.

Italian Wines and Food

Sommeliers have a general rule when it comes to pairing food and wine: What grows together goes together. This holds particularly true for Italian wines. If you've dined in a trattoria in Montalcino, you probably noticed that not only is the list full of Brunellos but it is almost exclusively Tuscan as well. It's not just local pride; it's because the wines pair exquisitely with the local fare. If you have had a glass of Brunello with *ravioli al sugo di cinghiale* (local wild boar ravioli) you understand. The wine and cuisine have evolved hand in hand. Wine breathes life into the glass and its consumption can lead to a euphoria that has nothing—okay, perhaps a little— to do with the alcohol. Most waiters will be happy to suggest the best pairings; however, I will highlight those that absolutely must not be missed in the Classic Wines and Classic Pairings suggestions, which are listed separately according to province in the sections covering Northern, Central, and Southern Italy.

MR. & MRS. ITALY'S CERTIFIED SOMMELIER

Mr. & Mrs. Italy are honored to include Caleb Hopkins, with his vast knowledge of oenology, as a member of its editorial team. He is a certified sommelier with the Court of Master Sommeliers, and for over a decade has worked in beverage management throughout the United States, including Hawaii. He regularly competes in sommelier competitions, recently taking home top honors among nine sommeliers in a blind wine-tasting competition known as the Annual Man (or Woman!) vs. Wine. He has also been a wine judge for the Pacific Northwest Wine competition in Oregon. Last year he joined Atlas restaurant at the St. Regis Atlanta, where he works closely with chef Christopher Grossman to perfect their international wine list. Caleb travels throughout Europe regularly in order to immerse himself in its many diverse wine regions, but Italy is surely one of his favorite spots.

A Culinary Journey through Italy

Italy is home to exceptional and important museums, ancient ruins, and medieval castles, but there is no doubt that some of its greatest pleasures are to be experienced through its sensational cuisine.

This book is dedicated to helping you explore Italy from an epicurean's perspective, not by recommending individual restaurants but by highlighting those properties we feel exemplify an exciting new trend in travel: the luxury hotel as culinary destination.

No doubt Italy is famous as a gourmand's delight. In fact, one of the highlights of traveling through Italy is the diversity of ingredients and food preparation methods found throughout the regions, all deeply influenced by their past and revealing their own individual gastronomic traditions. Italian cuisine is symbolic of a country that wasn't unified until 1861. Previously, each region produced only its classic cuisine, relying solely on ingredients that could be harvested and cultivated locally. Today, regional products can be shipped all over Italy, but Italians still stay true to their locally produced ingredients, as they choose freshness and quality over a multiplicity of ingredients or the latest culinary trends. Therefore, classic Italian cuisine can only be categorized by one common denominator: incorporation of top-quality ingredients that are omnipresent throughout the country.

As Italy's regional climates and geographical conditions are different from one another, the available products as well as the tastes of the people vary; consequently, recipes that originated in one particular region will have an entirely different style and flavor when prepared in another. Pasta certainly is typical of Italian cuisine, yet each region has its own unique shape and preparation, such as the *trenette* of the Ligurian coast, the *tortellini* of Emilia-Romagna, or the *tagliatelle* of Umbria.

The heart of Italian cooking today is still its simplicity; ingredients are used to complement rather than mask the taste of the fresh vegetables, fruits, meats, fish, and even cheeses. For instance, along the seaside, freshly caught fish is usually grilled and then served with a touch of olive oil, lemon, and freshly ground pepper. The succulent blood oranges from Sicily as prepared in *insalata di arance* (orange salad) need nothing more than a little fresh raw fennel, onions, rosemary, ground pepper, and oil and vinegar as accompaniments. Even pasta is intended to be served with sauces that enhance, not distract from, the pureness of its flavor.

Italian desserts are completely delectable, yet the ingredients blend together so perfectly their parts are indistinguishable from the whole. A good example of this is panna cotta, the famous upside-down whipped cream pudding of Emilia-Romagna,

ABOVE: Pizza, pasta, and gelato: kids of all ages love Italian food, and learning to cook it is a super fun way for them to immerse themselves in the culture. Trullalleri Kid's Club at the luxurious Borgo Egnazia, Brindisi, offers a host of fun activities for their little guests.

OPPOSITE: Romantik Hotel Turm's owner and award-winning chef Stefan Pramstrahler is a master of the art of interpreting local South Tyrolean cuisine in an original and flavorsome way. Restaurant Turm is guaranteed to satisfy the most discriminating palates.

which is made with only cream, vanilla bean, gelatin, and sugar as the backdrop to fresh raspberries and strawberries.

Many of the hotels and cafes will advertise American breakfast because *colazione* (Italian breakfast) is quite different. *Colazione* is light, and traditionally consists of cappuccino (concentrated coffee with frothed milk) and a brioche (sweet pastry) or just simply an espresso (concentrated coffee). Customarily, *pranzo* (lunch) is the largest meal of the day. A traditional Italian meal is orchestrated like a great theatrical production, with a series of scenes presented in a succinct order: *antipasto* (starter), a *primo piatto* (pasta, rice, or soup), a *secondo piatto* (meat or fish) with *contorno* (vegetable or salad), then *frutta* (fresh fruit). *Cena* (dinner) is similar to lunch. Today there is a trend toward having a light lunch, with dinner as the main meal. Both meals may be finished with espresso and maybe a grappa, amaro, Vin Santo or limoncello (digestive liqueurs).

In addition to their restaurants, many of our properties also support on-site gardens, olive groves, and vineyards. A few are even located on or near working farms. As such, in many cases guests are able to buy these locally produced foodstuffs, as well as other regional delicacies, in addition to enjoying them at mealtimes. If you do so, you may notice certain foods such as cheeses and sausages carry a special government-approved seal, which acknowledges its outstanding regional quality. This is known as the "controlled designation of origin," indicated by the initials DOC. Foods that receive this stamp of approval have met the government's strictest of standards for quality and authenticity. A prime example is Asiago cheese from the Veneto region. Asiago received its DOC certification in 1978, which not only limited the geographical area in which the milk used in its production could be produced and collected but also ensured that its traditional production methods were adhered to and carried out. The officially recognized zones are defined as the whole province of Vicenza and Trento, as well as the two provinces of Treviso and Padova. Asiago also received an additional certification of DOP, or "protected designation of origin," one of only thirty among Italy's four hundred or so cheeses to have been awarded this honor.

Regardless of its simplicity or sophistication, whether the products were collected and produced in Piedmonte or Puglia, or if its ingredients hold a DOC or DOP certification, Italian cuisine ultimately arouses the senses though its artful expression and the joining together of friends and family.

Dining Out in Italy

All in all, our featured hotels and resorts offer some of the finest award-winning cuisine and dining experiences available in Italy. While all the properties featured in this book were chosen because of their culinary excellence, there are a few that we feel worthy of special mention. In these cases, we have written expanded reviews with more in depth information, which you can find in their corresponding sections—Northern, Central, or Southern Italy.

Liech.

Switzerland

Austria

Bressanone

Trentino-Alto Adige

Bolzano

Cortina d'Ampezzo

Friuli-Venezia Giulia

Lago Maggiore
Verbania
Stresa

Sondrio

Belluno

Pordenone

Udine

Slovenia

Trento

Lago di Como

Lombardia

Riva del Garda

Gorizia

Rivarotta di Pasiano

Valle d'Aosta

Varese

Como

Lecco

Veneto

Aosta

Cogne

Azzate

Bergamo

Lago
di Garda

Bassano
del Grappa

Treviso

Biella

Vizzola
Ticino

Monza e Brianza

Erbusco

Corrubbio Di San
Pietro In Cariano

Vicenza

Mira Porte

France

Ivrea

Novara

Milan

Brescia

Verona

Padova

Trieste

Vercelli

Piedmonte

Pavia

Lodi

Cremona

Venice

Croatia

Turin

Mantova

Rovigo

Asti

Alessandria

Cuneo

Liguria

Genoa

Camogli

Portofino Vetta

Savona

Cinque
Terre

La Spezia

Imperia

San Remo

Northern Italy

With its diversity of landscapes and cultures, northern Italy has long been a favorite destination for the adventurous traveler. Within only a few days' time, you can ski towering alpine peaks, navigate the labyrinthine canals of Venice, scout the chic boutiques of Milan, and lounge in luxury at exclusive resorts along the Ligurian Coast. Grand palaces, medieval castles, and innumerable artistic treasures from antiquity to the present day await the intrepid traveler. Food and wine aficionados will have many opportunities to indulge their passions. French and German influences have left their mark not only on the region's wine-making traditions but also on the culinary styles, which range from down home to haute cuisine.

Valle d'Aosta

This region is positioned in the northwestern corner of Italy, and is the country's most mountainous area, entirely surrounded by impressive alpine peaks: Monte Blanc, the Matterhorn, the Monte Rosa, and the Gran Paradiso. Aosta, capital of the region and the only province of the valley, is a city rich in history; the ancient Augusta Pretoria (Latin name for Aosta) is evident in the great Arch of Augustus (25 B.C.) and the remains of the Roman Theatre. It is also one of the best towns from which to explore the mountains and valleys, which offer great hiking, biking, paddling, climbing, and skiing opportunities. The main resorts of the area are Courmayeur and Cervinia, which extends over the border into Switzerland. Others present stunning surroundings along with interesting *pistes* (ski runs) for skiers of all levels. Such destinations include Pila, which is accessible from the town of Aosta by gondola, Gressonney, Champoluc, Alagna, and Valtournenche. This vast snowy area begins at 1,524 meters and eventually climbs to 4,478 meters to the top of the Matterhorn. This region is an enchanting paradise of feudal castles and towers from the Middle Ages, particularly along the Dora Baltea River.

The mountain resort town of Saint-Vincent is a great base from which to tour the many castles of Valle d'Aosta, Casino de la Vallée (one of Europe's largest casinos), mineral water spas, the nearby mountains, and Italy's oldest park, Gran Paradiso National Park. Cogne is one of the most beautiful summer mountain

Bellevue Hotel & Spa, located in Valle d'Aosta, is the perfect spot for a getaway year round. It is especially suited for nature enthusiasts and lovers of outdoor sports such as cross country skiing, walking, and ice climbing, which are abundant throughout the area.

villages of the Alps with many inspiring walks and hikes of various degrees of difficulty, leading to lakes and waterfalls. In the winter Cogne offers cross-country and some downhill skiing, snowshoeing, and more than 140 icefalls for ice climbing.

Classic Cuisine: The cuisine of northern Italy has been influenced by the close proximity of both France and Piedmonte, but maintains its own distinguished character. Rich in dairy products, the region's cuisine functions to generate heat in the alpine climate. Specialties include mushrooms, roasted meats, and cheeses, of which Fontina, produced in the region since the 12th century, is the best known. The Northern Italian version of cheese fondue is a *fonduta,* made with melted Fontina, milk, eggs, and flour. Other local specialties include nourishing soups, stews, risotto, and polenta, as well as *Costoletta alla Valdostana*, a veal chop covered in Fontina.

Classic Wines: As you can imagine, the smallest region in Italy produces the least amount of wine, the vast majority of which is consumed within its seven subregions. One of the most popular wines, and especially enjoyable after a day on the slopes, is the sparkling Blanc de Morgex et de la Salle Spumante. For a truly indulgent experience, try the exotically perfumed Chambave Muscat Fletri, a dessert wine made from the Moscato Bianco grape.

Classic Pairings: To accompany the famed fontina cheese, or fontina-based stews, you must sample the reds of Donnas, made from the Nebbiolo grape. Being lighter in style, they deliver red fruit notes and a tartness to balance the richness of the cheese.

Piedmonte

Like the Valle d'Aosta, this region's appeal lies in its proximity to beautiful alpine landscapes and to France, which has an abundant influence on the region's culinary output. Piedmonte is also an outdoor adventurer's dream, with superb hiking and mountain biking opportunities. Its portion of the Italian lakes includes Lake Orta and the whole western half of Lake Maggiore. Turin, the capital, is a fascinating European city, boasting both a contemporary international flavor and an aura of antiquity. It is home to the much-disputed reproduction of the Holy Shroud in which Jesus was allegedly wrapped after he was removed from the cross. It can be seen on display in the Cathedral of San Giovanni. In Turin, you will also find the Egyptian Museum, holding one of the most important collections of Egyptian artifacts existing outside of Egypt itself. Other noteworthy sites include the extensive weaponry collection housed at the Royal Armory; important

Piemontese, Dutch, and Flemish artwork at the Sabauda Gallery; the Automotive Museum's collection of cars ranging from vintage to modern and concept; the Royal Palace, built in the 17th century to house the House of Savoy; and the Mole Antonelliana, a major landmark built in 1863 as a synagogue that now houses the National Museum of Cinema. Stresa, previously a small fishing village, has developed into a popular tourist area located on one of the most scenic areas of Lake Maggiore. Castles are plentiful throughout the region, lending a fairytale characteristic to their surroundings.

Classic Cuisine: The region's highly prized, rare, and very costly *tartufi bianchi* (white truffles) that grow underground beneath certain oak trees attract food connoisseurs from all over the world. Production is concentrated in and around the small town of Alba, and the fungi are utilized not only in specialty food items like truffle-scented olive oils and truffle-infused cheeses, but also by the world's finest chefs to enrich a variety of pastas, risottos, and meats. Piedmonte is also home to the prized porcini mushroom, which is prevalent in many local dishes. A popular meal is *fonduta*, a melted cheese dip of milk, eggs, and the famous white truffles. *Bagna Cauda* is a raw vegetable fondue with hot anchovy dip and, of course, white truffles. Other regional favorites include game such as rabbit and boiled meat dishes like *Vitello Tonnato*, which is veal with tuna sauce. Piedmonte offers a multitude of high-quality cheeses, which include the flavorful Gorgonzola, Taleggio, Grana Padano, and Castelmagno, a time-honored cheese of exceptional quality produced in very small quantities.

Classic Wines: Piedmont has long been considered the Burgundy of Italy. It is certainly one of the country's most important regions for the vine. With sixteen separate DOCGs, its contribution is massive. Three major red grapes are Nebbiolo, Barbera, and Dolcetto. Dolcetto, which means "sweet little one," produces light and fruit-driven wines. Look for the producers Chionetti and Ca' Viola. Barbera is the most planted red grape in this region. It can produce some amazing wines for a great value. Both Vietti and Prunotto make good examples. Braids di Giacomo Bologna makes Bricco dell'Uccellone, which shows Barbera's far more serious side.

The two stars of Piedmont are certainly Barolo and Barbaresco. Barolo is a wine of stunning depth, richness, and structure. There are so many great producers that it is difficult to narrow them down to just a few, but here are some to look for: Bartolo Mascarello, Giuseppe Rinaldi, Giacomo Conterno, Ceretto, Bruno Giacosa, Giuseppe Mascarello, Elio Altare, and Aldo Conterno.

If Barolo is king, then Barbaresco is queen. As a rule it also produces a lighter wine. Most of the producers listed above make Barbaresco wines as well, but one of the finest is Angelo Gaja. The Produttori del Barbaresco, a cooperative founded by the town's priest in 1958, makes consistently great wine. The first white DOCG was Cortese di Gavi. These wines are popular for their great mineral notes.

Piedmont also produces quality sparkling wine. Asti/Moscato d'Asti DOCG is made from the Moscato Bianco grape. It is the largest DOC producer in the whole of Italy.

Classic Pairings: Barbera is tremendously versatile. It classically goes with wild game, such as rabbit, and with the lighter Piedmontese cheeses. For richer stewed meats, a bold Barolo can be a strong, yet pleasant, enhancement.

Liguria

Liguria is a narrow strip of land, encircled by the Mediterranean Sea, the Maritime Alps, and the Apennines mountains. Its flora and fauna are among the most diverse and interesting in Italy. Liguria's natural, rich beauty has inspired an array of endearing names such as "Paradise Gulf," "Siren Bay," "Bay of Silence," "Bay of Fairy Tales," and "Sea's Echo." The coastline is geographically divided between the Western Riviera and the Eastern Riviera. Serving as the region's capital and center point, the city of Genoa divides the region into the *Riviera di Ponente*, which extends west to the French border and is characterized by long sand and pebble beaches, and the *Riviera di Levante*. This beautiful stretch of coastline begins with smooth, sandy beaches, climbs magnificently precipitous jagged cliffs, and then rolls into the peaks of the Appennines. Sanremo is the crown jewel of the *Riviera di Ponente* and one of the most esteemed spots of Liguria. The city is Italy's flower capital and owes its fame primarily to the *Festival della Canzone* (Italian music competition). Nonetheless, its glamorous boutiques and ancient village are not to be underestimated. The *Riviera di Levante* boasts cities whose names are internationally renowned. The

Tigullio Gulf includes Rapallo, Sestri, Portofino, and Camogli, which perhaps remains the most authentic of the towns. Further south sits the breathtaking charm of the Cinque Terre, five small towns each with their own particular allure, perched along the coast's cliffs. At the end of the Riviera is the *Golfo dei Poeti* (Poets Gulf), which includes the towns of Lerici and Portovenere.

Classic Cuisine: The basis of all recipes is olive oil, and the most well-known is the basil *pesto* sauce, traditionally served as *trenette col pesto* with its main ingredients of fresh basil, pine nuts, olive oil, garlic, and Parmesan cheese. There are a wide variety of *ravioli*; the most typical is *pansotti con salsa di noci*, filled with Swiss chard, basil, Ricotta, and Parmesan cheese with a walnut sauce. Ligurian pies are perhaps the most flavorful, from the simple *focaccia* with oil and salt, to *torta pasqualina,* a savory Easter pie with layers of pastry filled with spinach, egg, herbs, ricotta, and *Parmigiano* cheese. Veal is one of the most commonly used meats and includes recipes such as *Cima ripiena alla Genovese,* which is stuffed breasts of veal with vegetables, herbs, pine nuts, and Parmesan cheese. But fish like cod, sardines, mullet, tuna, swordfish, sea bass, squid, and especially anchovies are the most revered on the Ligurian coast and are served in a variety of ways: in soups and stews, as a *fritti misti* (mixed selection fried), or as a fish salad. Mussels are a popular dish, typically served as *zuppa di cozze* (mussel soup). Ligurians are fond of vegetables as well, particularly those that can be stuffed, like *fiori di zucchini ripieni* (Stuffed zucchini blossoms). Their desserts are simple and often fried, like *ravioli dolci* (sweet ravioli).

Classic Wines: This region follows the coast. The staggering heights of the cliff-side vineyards instantly inspire respect for the courage of the winemaker. The Vermentino-based whites are light and refreshing, with a hint of green herbs. These delightful wines are perfect for sipping, whether on a leisurely boating excursion or on the terrace after a day spent hiking the Cinque Terre, feet up, glass in hand, watching the sun melt into the ocean.

Classic Pairings: The bright herbal notes of the Vermentino-based whites also make them a great match for the special pesto found throughout this region.

Lombardy

Nestled in the middle of northern Italy, with the Swiss Alps forming part of its northernmost borders, Lombardy comprises the main section of the Po River Valley and is one of Italy's busiest commercial-industrial regions. As Lombardy's capital and its largest city, Milan is a modern, prosperous city, and hosts the Italian headquarters of many banks and corporations. It is also renowned, along with Paris and New York, as a major center of fashion and design. Blending the old and the new, Milan has many points of interest, including impressive cathedrals like the Duomo di Milano (locally referred to as Il Duomo), incredible designer shopping and boutiques, La Scala (a world-renowned opera house), Leonardo's The Last Supper in the church of Santa Maria delle Grazie, and the enchanting Navigli district, whose canals play host to the city's young crowd in numerous entertaining bars and restaurants. Milan is also home to one of the world's most important exhibitions of contemporary and innovative short films, drawing filmmakers and

viewers from around the globe each September. Lake Como is a favorite vacation spot for Europeans, thanks to its combination of fine art, gorgeous scenery, and invigorating mountain air. From here, you can take a relaxing boat trip to view the many noble villas and gardens, or venture to the charming villages of Bellagio, Tremezzo, and Varenna. Piazza Cavour, in the town of Lake Como, has lakeside cafes and fashionable shopping boutiques, as well as breathtaking views of the snow-capped Alps. Nearby is Lake Maggiore, with its three islands: Isola Bella, Isola dei Pescatori, and Isola Madre. Three other Lombardy towns deserving a visit are Bergamo, with its Piazza Vecchia, considered one of the most picturesque squares in all of Italy; Mantova's Ducal Palace, with its series of frescoes by Mantegna; and Cremona, home to the master artisan of stringed instruments, Stradivari. In line with the region's natural beauty and popularity of outdoor activities, golf courses in this region are considered some of Italy's most beautiful.

Classic Cuisine: Visitors will find Lombardy to be exceptionally diverse in the culinary realm. Each city has its own gastronomic history and style. Milan, in particular, seems to be a freethinking city, and consequently, more inclined to contemporary cuisine in which specialties from different Italian regions are merged

with local dishes. Lombardy is known for its rice dishes, the most common being *Risotto alla Milanese*, which is a creamy saffron short-grain rice, blended with meat or chicken stock, onion, pepper and Parmesan cheese. One of the region's favorite pastas is pumpkin *tortelli* from Mantua, but the *Ossobuco* (stewed veal shank) still remains a traditional main course. Other distinctive ingredients include olive oil, freshly cured meats, and remarkable cheeses, such as the richly flavored Gorgonzola, Crescenza, Grano Padano, Mascarpone (primarily used to make desserts and mousses), and Bito, which has been in existence since the start of the 11th century.

Classic Wines: One of the most important DOCGs in this region is Franciacorta, whose wines are made in the same method as Champagne. A number of them compete on quality, including the Ca' Del Boscos's prestige cuvee, Annamaria Clementi, which is made only during a perfect grape-growing season. It is one of the finest expressions of the sparkling style. Bella Vista makes a vintage dated bottling called Satèn, which means "made from white grapes." This bottling is 100 percent Chardonnay, and offers a wonderful show of depth. Citrus fruits, peach blossoms, and a golden honey finish are on full display.

Classic Pairings: Franciacorta's Bruts pair perfectly with cured meats or dry cheeses. For a richer dish, like risotto, try one of the Satèn styles.

Trentino–Alto Adige

This area along Italy's northeastern border with Austria is a spectacular territory of jagged ridges and snow-capped peaks, sparkling waterfalls and sweeping meadows, fabulous ski resorts and enchanting medieval towns. In winter, the skiing is absolutely first rate. Spring and fall offer captivating hikes and climbs along a wide range of well-marked trails with stops in distant mountain hamlets. Castles abound, and many are open to visitors; some have even been transformed into hotels and restaurants. As the name suggests, Trentino–Alto Adige is split into two provinces: Trentino in the south is mostly Italian speaking and includes the towns of Trento, Rovereto, Madonna di Campiglio, and Riva del Garda. Südtirol or South Tyrol, the northern area of Alto Adige, includes Bolzano, Bressanone, and Merano. Italy annexed South Tyrol in 1919; it was previously part of Austria-Hungary, hence the prevalence of German speakers. For lovers of culture and history, this area has much to offer with numerous historic sites, museums, and important monuments. The city of Bozen remains to this day predominantly German, and thus is a showcase for many aspects of that culture, including the South Tyrol Museum of Archaeology, where the five-thousand-year-old "Iceman," discovered in 1991, is housed. Brixen/Bressanone is the main town of the valley, which exudes artistic and historical riches and a special charm. The Plose Mountain soars over the town and is a prominent ski resort. Meran/Merano is famous for its parks, gardens, promenades, footpaths, and medieval town center. Trento/Trentino stands at the crossroads of Italian and Northern European cultures. Visit the Castello del Buonconsiglio, the castle that was home to the prince bishops of Trento for many centuries, as well as the *duomo* with its splendid square.

Classic Cuisine: Trentino–Alto Adige shares culinary traditions with both the Italian and German sides of its border. The staples are polenta (corn meal), prepared in various ways, along with wild fowl, river trout, sauerkraut, and smoked meat, particularly local *speck* (juniper-flavored prosciutto). A favorite dish throughout Trentino–Alto Adige, *canederli* are gnocchi (dump-lings) made from bread and flour and served in a broth. Mushrooms are plentiful and are used to make thick, flavorful sauces served with polenta, pasta, and, most commonly, meat dishes. Vegetables used are primarily beets, cabbage, potatoes, and turnips. The region's apples are full of flavor, making traditional strudels irresistible. *Zelten,* a mixture of yeast, flour, milk, sugar, butter, walnuts, dried figs, sultanas (golden raisins), pine nuts, and candied fruit, was once eaten only at Christmas. As the symbolic dessert of the region, today it is sold year round in pastry shops. The region's most important cheese is Grana Trentino, although Grana Padano DOP and Asiago DOP may also be made in the province. Each Alpine village makes its own variety called *nostrano* (our own).

Classic Wines: In this region, the German style is obvious. Many wines are labeled by varietal. Valle Isarco, a subzone of Alto Adige, shows promise with its Veltliner, Silverner and Kerner. They additionally produce impressive expressions of Sauvignon Blanc, called, simply, Sauvignon. After a full day of hitting the slopes, you may prefer something with a little more body. In which case, Franz Haas produces a "Schweizer" Pinot Nero that is ripe and opulent without sacrificing precision.

Classic Pairings: Speck, a local specialty, pairs well with a Sauvignon or with a Pinot Grigio. A crisp Pinot Nero's bright acidity will cut through the doughy texture of gnocchi, leaving a perfect marriage of flavors.

Veneto

This area is a hidden treasure and relatively unpopulated with tourists. Most people associate this region with Venice, a fascinating city of labyrinthine canals and alleyways, charming homes, notable villas, and impressive squares with stately buildings. The Jewish ghetto of Venice is an extraordinary and unique quarter with five synagogues (15th to 16th century) and ancient pawnshops. To venture no farther than Venice, however, would be to miss so many other magnificent locales of this region. Verona, for instance, is one of Veneto's most eye-catching and historical cities. It is home to the Capulet house with Juliet's legendary balcony, outstanding Roman ruins, and magnificent examples of Medieval and Renaissance buildings. The city is full of music, and its piazzas and streets are especially festive during the annual summer opera festival held in the Roman Arena. Vicenza is an essential visit for any lover of architecture. Andrea Palladio moved here as a child and has, without a doubt, left his mark throughout the city. He is known for a fundamental use of column rows and a harmonization of his work in accordance with the surrounding land. In Padua, one can also appreciate works by Medieval and Renaissance artists, of whom Giotto's frescoes are perhaps the most important. Valpolicella is a fertile valley covered with innumerable family wineries that offer enchanting countryside and never-ending panoramas. Fifteenth-century walls surround Treviso, perfectly safeguarding its remarkable architectural and artistic masterpieces. Abano, a thermal spa town located in the center of this region, has hot water springs that have drawn visitors since Roman times. Chioggia, a mini-Venice with picturesque canals and busy riverbanks, is alive with people buying fish and vegetables in the markets. Bassano del Grappa is renowned for its centuries-old production of grappa and handcrafted ceramics, its Palladian covered wooden bridge, and wonderful shops. Lake Garda, surrounded by the Alps, is perfect for windsurfing, sailing, and canoeing, as well as for yachting and fishing. In Marostica every second Friday, Saturday, and Sunday in September of an even-numbered year, you can watch a human chess game whose pieces are dressed in Renaissance costume. The game has been played this way since 1454, when Marostica belonged to the Venetian Republic. Few places are more picturesque than Cortina d'Ampezzo, one of Europe's chicest ski resorts.

Classic Cuisine: The cuisine of Venice is traditionally herb-and-spice-based, a tradition that goes back to the days when the European spice trade was controlled from the city. The cuisine is mainly polenta (corn meal) and rice, along with assorted shellfish, fresh fish, wild fowl, and mushrooms. Typical courses

include *risotto nero* (black squid risotto), *Fegato alla Veneziana* (pan-fried calf's liver) and radicchio, red chicory most often served grilled or as a salad. Venetian cooks masterfully combine various ingredients and create sauces that enhance original flavors. The unusual *Asparagi di Bassano* (white asparagus of Bassano), prepared in a variety of ways, is legendary. Italians have been making an incredible array of cured meats for thousands of years, and in the Veneto, pork with the addition of chicken liver or veal is most prevalent. Asiago DOC/DOP is the finest cheese, while tiramisu is the most renowned dessert of the region.

Classic Wines: The Veneto region conjures up visions of gondolas, but equally well-known are the wines produced just outside of Verona. Amarone della Valpolicella is one of the most interesting wines in Italy, and Masi, Alligrini, Tedeschi, and Giuseppe Quintarelli are just a few of its many great producers. For whites,

make sure to sample Soave Superiore DOCG, made from Garganega-based blends. The Conegliano Valdobbiadene Prosecco DOCG produces the other of Italy's famous sparking wines. Sipping a glass while sitting at one of Verona's medieval fountains is a wonderful experience. While in Venice, you must visit your hotel bar or a nearby café and order a Bellini, the signature drink of Venice. You may even try one in Harry's Bar, where the drink, Prosecco with a dollop of sweet fruit puree, was created.

Classic Pairings: Prosecco is a great food wine, being light and not too heavily sparkling. Pair it with cured meats, polenta in light sauces, and Venetian-style finger sandwiches.

Friuli Venezia Giulia

Situated in Italy's northeastern corner, Friuli is close to Austria, Slovenia, and Croatia. Though not often mentioned in guidebooks, Friuli is a diverse region teeming with beaches, secluded alpine villages, Roman ruins, splendid country villas, snow-capped mountains, rocky seaside cliffs, seaports, and picturesque fishing villages. Trieste, the area's primary sightseeing destination, is home to the Cathedral of San Giusto, with two Romanesque basilicas that were united in the 14th century. If you are interested in archaeology, the arch of Riccardo (33 B.C.) and the Roman theatre (1st and 2nd centuries A.D.) are inspiring sites. Triste's Giuseppe Verdi theatre hosts its famed opera season, in addition to the International Operetta Festival. Extending out into the sea, the wonderfully preserved medieval Castle of Miramare features grounds with English and Italian gardens, unusual plants, sculptures, and ponds. In Gorizia, the esteemed Attems Petzenstein Palace houses an art museum and the Museum of the Synagogue. Along with documentation on the history of the Jewish community, paintings of the poet and philosopher Carlo Michelstaedter are on display. The Marano Lagoon is home to countless migrating waterfowl, while Grado is a village composed of narrow streets reminiscent of Venice's smaller canals and pathways. This ancient fishing village is adjacent to a beach resort and a well-known health spa.

game. Trieste and Grado culinary styles are influenced by the Venetian manner of preparing seafood, with definitive Slavic and Austrian flavors. Typical favorites, especially around Trieste, are *Iota*, a bean, potato, and white cabbage soup; *Porcina*, a mix of boiled pork with sauerkraut, mustard, and horseradish; and a Slavic-style goulash and dumplings. Seafood, including turbot, sardines, prawns, cuttlefish, squid, scallops, crabs, and eels, is favored along the coastline. Montasio DOP cheese has been an export of the region since the 18th century, and can only be produced legally within Friuli Venezia-Giulia and certain Veneto provinces. Some typical desserts are German-style apple strudel and *crostoli*, a fried dough.

Classic Cuisine: Polenta (corn meal) is the food most often found on a table in Friuli, and is often accompanied by flavorsome sauces, game, chicken, rabbit, or salted cheeses such as *frico*, fried in butter. Soups are typically made with beans, greens, or pork ribs, and a plentiful serving of lard. *Prosciutto di San Daniele* DOP is considered one of the world's best hams, made only by twenty-seven small producers within the town of San Daniele. The woodlands are abundant with mushrooms, herbs, fruit crops, and

Classic Wines: This region is known for crisp, bright whites that should be drunk young. The region's most noted native white varietal is Friulano. Alternatively, two DOCGs are Colli Orientali del Friuli Picolit and Ramandolo, both of which produce lovely sweet dessert wines using native grapes.

Classic Pairings: The famous Prosciutto di San Daniele DOP is perfectly matched with a glass of the native Friulano, whose bright fruits cut right through the richness and salinity of the ham.

BELLEVUE HOTEL & SPA

Rue Grand Paradis, 22 | 11012 Cogne (Vallée d'Aoste) | Italy
Tel: +39 016574825 | Fax: +39 0165749192
E-mail: info@hotelbellevue.it
Website: www.hotelbellevue.it

BELLEVUE HOTEL & SPA is located in Valle d'Aosta, one of the most splendid and picturesque regions of Italy, bordering both Switzerland and France. A member of the Relais & Chateaux and Historical Italian Sites, the hotel and spa is surrounded by breathtaking views of the Prateria dell'Orso and is opposite a glacier in the heart of the Gran Paradiso national park in the center of Cogne. The property continues to be lovingly run by the Jeantet Roullet family, who has welcomed guests for four generations. A harmonic balance of rustic charm and sophisticated elegance was achieved through the careful renovation of this ancient alpine lodge, which still conveys its historical and antique atmosphere. This is the perfect spot for a getaway year round, especially for nature enthusiasts and lovers of outdoor sports such as cross country skiing, walking, and ice climbing, which are abundant throughout the area. The Gran Paradiso Springs, which in November 2013 was awarded the Prix Villégiature as Best Hotel Spa in Europe, features 12,000 square feet of aquatic and wellness paths amid the beautiful Santi Orso fields, two indoor swimming pools, a whirlpool bath, five perfumed saunas, two steam baths, a salt grotto, an ice grotto, a fitness area, and several relaxation rooms. The oasis not only offers a wide range of wellness and relaxation treatments, but also romantic treatments for couples, such as Bear's Grotto, King Victor's Bath, or the Marmot's Den. Under the superb artistic talent of Chef Fabio Iacovone, a variety of eateries offer guests regional and international cuisine, including: the one-star Bellevue, the Bar à Fromage, Restaurant de Montagne; and La Brasserie du Bon Bec, which is located in the main square of Cogne, just steps from the hotel. All feature vegetables, fruits, and herbs grown at the hotel's on-site organic garden. Once a week during the summer, a barbeque is organized in the on-site mountain hut, which is a very special experience.

FINE POINTS

Rooms: 28 rooms plus 7 suites with Jacuzzi's, fireplaces, and some with private saunas; 3 chalets with fireplaces. One panoramic suite, the Angel's Nest, offers 180-degree views of the Sant'Orso fields, and spacious living, sleeping, and bathing accommodations.

Food: La Terrazza (lunchtime à la carte), Bellevue restaurant and Le Petit Restaurant, Bar à Fromage, Restaurant de Montagne, La Brasserie du Bon Bec, cheese cellar, and wine cellar with over 1,300 vintages.

Special Features: Gran Paradiso Springs spa; summer excursions include free climbing, mountaineering, mountain biking, fishing, tennis, mini-golf, alpine guides, horseback riding, and weekly barbeque in mountain hut; winter excursions include cross-country skiing, alpine skiing, snow walks, snow rackets, ice falls, ski mountaineering, and horse carriage rides; year round excursions include nature guides, museums, castles, parks, waterfalls, lace production, cable crossing of Mount Blanc, panoramic flights, and a visit to the 56-meter-high, 50-meter-long Pont d'Ael Roman bridge.

CASTADIVA RESORT & SPA

Via Caronti, 69 | 22020 – Blevio (Lake Como) | Italy

Tel: +39 03132511

E-mail: info@castadivaresort.com

Website: www.castadivaresort.com

CASTADIVA RESORT & SPA is a new concept in lifestyle travel that offers its clientele the ultimate vacation experience. Occupying a majestic spot on the east side of Lake Como in the lovely village of Blevio, it is minutes away from the town of Como and a forty-five-minute drive from Milano Malpensa International Airport. Situated on a lush botanical park, it is truly a magnificent spot for a romantic vacation, epitomizing the qualities that for centuries have drawn discerning travelers to the region: luxury pampering, a wealth of recreational activities, and breathtaking natural surroundings. The core of CastaDiva is the nineteenth-cenury Villa Roccabruna, once home to the famous opera singer and Bellini muse, Guiditta Pasta. Today, it has been renovated into a luxurious five-star resort, the first to be built on Lake Como in over 100 years. In addition to the main resort, with its seventy-three rooms and suites, CastaDiva welcomes guests to stay in a series of small homes and villas that dot the property. Throughout, one will find the usual amenities available at a property of this caliber, along with personalized touches like Villeroy and Boch soaking tubs, a pillow and sheet "menu" from which guests can customize their materials and fabrics, and bath products created by a Florentine perfumer especially for the resort. This region is renowned for its spas and wellness treatments and CastaDiva is no exception. It offers the ultimate indulgence at the resort's pool, which is situated on a platform right on the lake, and at the CastaDiva Concept Spa, with its tailor-made approach to restoring balance and wellness that include four VIP rooms offering treatments inspired by the four elements: earth, water, air, and fire. The resort's gastronomic creations are showcased at L'Orangerie restaurant, which in 2016 announced its partnership with the two-Michelin-starred chef Gennaro Esposito. Esposito, an expert in Neapolitan cuisine who has worked in some of the most renowned restaurants in Europe and Italy, has crafted a menu of modern and classic Italian dishes that can be enjoyed during dinner by candlelight, out on the terrace, or in the privacy of one's room.

FINE POINTS

Rooms: 73 rooms and suites; 9 villas.

Food: Breakfast, lunch, and dinner at L'Orangerie; drinks and pastries at the Bellini Bar; spa cuisine for breakfast, lunch, and dinner at the Spa Café.

Special Features: CastaDiva Concept Spa with host of treatments plus ice room, salt room, Turkish and Mediterranean baths, Jacuzzi, and indoor pool; opera at nearby Como Opera House, in partnership with the resort; private boat tours of the lake on a vintage Riva craft; designer shopping across the border in Switzerland at Lugano's Fox Town outlet mall; golf, skiing, watercrafts, and whale watching all nearby; 24 hour front desk; babysitting services; business services; free Wi-Fi; air-conditioned throughout; banquet facilities.

CHALET DEL SOGNO

Mountain Experience Hotel | Via Spinale 37B - 38086 | Madonna di Campiglio, Italy
Tel: +39 0465441033 | Fax: +39 0465446605
E-mail: direzione@hotelchaletdelsogno.com
Website: www.hotelchaletdelsogno.com

CHALET DEL SOGNO offers an incredible opportunity to explore the very best of the stunning Brenta Dolomites mountain range. This hotel is run by the wonderfully warm and welcoming Schiavon family, who go above and beyond to ensure guests have an exceptional stay. Located in Madonna di Campiglio, a charming ski town that frequently hosts World Cup ski and snowboard races throughout the winter and the prestigious Giro d'Italia bike race in the summer, Chalet del Sogno is at the epicenter of mountain culture and elite athletic accomplishments. Here, some of the world's best alpine and Nordic skiing is literally just outside your door, as the hotel is walking distance from the chairlifts of Madonna di Campiglio, one of Italy's largest ski resorts. In the summer, the area offers world-class mountain biking, road biking, hiking, and rock climbing. The hotel itself was developed in accordance with sustainable building principles, with geothermal heating that significantly decreases carbon dioxide emissions. The spacious rooms, all suites, embody a tasteful mountain style in which to rest, and the gorgeous and extensive Oasi del Sogno wellness and fitness center features an indoor pool, Finnish sauna, and massage rooms, all perfect for unwinding after a day in the mountains. From the Due Pini Ristorante, which serves gourmet local cuisine accompanied by a rich selection of wines from the region and across Italy, to the gorgeous breakfast buffet, eating at Chalet del Sogno is a fantastic experience.

FINE POINTS

Rooms: 18 suites, including 3 luxury (approximately 500 square feet each), 2 junior (approximately 350 square feet each), and one comfort (approximately 475 square feet), and 1 two-room luxury (approximately 1,000 square feet), with two separate entrances and two bathrooms.

Food: Complimentary breakfast buffet with local meats, cheeses, yogurts, dry cereals, fresh and local eggs, fresh fruit, local honey, and fresh bread. Light dinner and aperitifs offered in the Stube, drinks and bar menu served in the Reading Room, and gourmet dinner served at Due Pini Ristorante.

Special Features: Full-service spa and fitness center, complete with indoor pool (outfitted with upstream swimming, water bikes, and water runners), fitness room, relaxation area with waterbeds and chromotherapy, infrared rays and vapor-hay Biosauna, Turkish bath, Finnish Sauna, and restorative treatments; Wi-Fi throughout hotel; complimentary parking; alpine guide available for hiking, trekking, and rock climbing; extensive mountain biking and road biking, with rentals available and personal tours from owner and Olympic athlete Alberto Schiavon.

CHÂTEAU MONFORT

Château Monfort Hotel (Relais & Chateaux)

Corso Concordia, 1 | 20129 Milano, Italy

Tel + 39 02776761 | Fax + 39 0277676832

E-mail monfort@relaischateaux.com

Website www.hotelchateaumonfort.com

CHÂTEAU MONFORT is more than just another luxury hotel. This is a home away from home, where guests can cozy up with a book or chat with travel companions and fellow guests in the common spaces like The Lounge Bar Mezzanotte, situated off the lobby under a stunning dome ceiling, or Alcova del Rubacuori. The on-site Amore & Psiche (Cupid and Psyche) SPA and fitness center is a place where you easily forget the commotion of everyday life and surrender yourself to moments of total bliss, particularly with an immersion in the tepid salt-water pool under chromatic healing lights. A member of the esteemed Planetaria Hotels of Italy, the Château Monfort not only fires the imagination but also delights with the very best in first-class amenities and attentive service. The ornately designed historic building is an architectural marvel of neo-Romantic art and décor, whose public spaces impart an air of Old World luxury and charm. Each of the seventy-seven rooms and suites are likewise designed to envelop guests in the romance of another place and time, while the junior suites are breathtakingly outfitted in décor inspired by one of five operas: L'Uccello di Fuoco, La Traviata, Madame Butterfly, Turandot, and Cinderella. Open April through October and located in the heart of Milan, the hotel is an ideal base from which to explore the city—the main fashion district as well at the Piazza Duomo, with its stunning fourteenth-century Gothic cathedral and expansive square, are only a few minute's walk away. Once back at the Château, your dining options include no less than three different themed rooms at the hotel's main restaurant, Rubacuori. Here, one can indulge in the most carefully prepared and authentic Italian dishes and Milanese specialties. The wine offerings come straight from the hotel's personal cellar, the elegant Cella di Bacco wine bar, where one can also book custom wine tastings.

FINE POINTS

Rooms: 77 superior, executive, and deluxe rooms; 5 suites.

Food: Breakfast, light lunch, and drinks at Bar Mezzanote; lunch and dinner at Rubacuori Restaurant; wine tastings at Cella di Bacco.

Special Features: All rooms feature state-of-the-art soundproofing, climate control, and audio/visual technologies, as well as all the comforts expected from a five-star hotel, including free high speed Internet service; Amore & Psiche SPA with Turkish bath/Hammam, sauna, and variety of massage and beautifying services; fitness center and swimming pool; meeting, banquet, and wedding facilities; pet friendly; 24-hour front desk; attentive concierge that excels at helping guests craft tailor-made itineraries, whether based on art, fashion, history, or cuisine; babysitting service; valet parking and airport transportation.

CRISTALLO HOTEL SPA & GOLF

Via R. Menardi 42 | 32043 Cortina d'Ampezzo (BL) | Dolomite, Italy

Tel: +39 0436881111 | Fax +39 0436870110

E-mail: info@cristallo.it

Website: www.cristallo.it

CRISTALLO HOTEL SPA & GOLF is the only five-star luxury hotel in the Dolomites, whose history of providing fine hospitality to discerning guests dates back to 1901, when Cortina began to emerge as one of Europe's premier resort destinations. Located only two hours from Venice, it offers maximum comfort, glamorous accommodations, state-of-the-art wellness and beauty treatments, world-class golf, four dining venues, and a cocktail bar. Set atop a hill and surrounded by spectacular towering mountains, Cristallo is truly a hotel for every season and style of adventure, whether skiing, golfing, hiking, or biking. Although you may be hard-pressed to leave the property—you could easily spend your entire sojourn at the expansive Transvital Swiss Beauty Center, soaking in the views from the covered pool, working out at the gym, or playing golf—a trip into Cortina for shopping and people-watching is a must, as is a winter skiing adventure or summer mountain trek. When it comes time to retire, you'll do so in rooms and suites offering spectacular views, hand-painted wall paneling, linens crafted from the finest cottons and silks, embroidered carpets, and Gustavian-style furniture and décor. Since its reopening in 2001, the Cristallo Hotel Spa & Golf has received numerous national and international awards, both for its accommodations and for its culinary offerings, which can be sampled at no less than four restaurants overseen by a masterful executive chef. Il Gazebo offers a refined menu of international gourmet cuisine; La Veranda del Cristallo excels in Italian specialties; La Stube 1872 serves authentic local dishes; and Il Cantuccio, the Chef's Private Table, offers multi-course wine-pairing dinners. A variety of specialty drinks, beer, wine, and, of course, the ever-famous Cristallo hospitality, is available at the cocktail bar.

FINE POINTS

Rooms: 74 rooms.

Food: 4 restaurants serving breakfast buffet, lunch, and dinner; 1 cocktail bar; room service.

Special Features: All rooms feature king-sized beds, hypoallergenic latex mattresses, flat screen LCD and digital satellite television, SKY TV decoder, high speed Internet, 2 telephone and fax lines, and hydro massage Jacuzzi tubs; swimming pool; fitness center with Technogym equipment; state-of-the art Transvital Swiss Beauty Center offering variety of massages, rejuvenating treatments, and cosmetics; business center; free Wi-Fi throughout the hotel; access to exclusive Cortina Golf Club; shuttle bus service into Cortina.

GRAND HOTEL TERME

Terme e Grandi Alberghi Sirmione SpA | Viale Marconi, 7 | 25019 Sirmione (BS), Italy

Tel: +39 0309904922

E-mail: booking@termedisirmione.com

Website: www.termedisirmione.com

GRAND HOTEL TERME has a 120-year history of attracting visitors from around the world with its compelling combination of beautiful natural surroundings, luxury accommodations, and unique thermal water, renowned for its preventive, therapeutic, and relaxation properties. Located just outside the historical center of Sirmione on Lake Garda, halfway between Milan and Venice, this five-star property is part of the Terme di Sirmione complex, a series of elegant hotels and state-of-the-art thermal centres that maximize the unique therapeutic benefits of the sulphurous salso-bromo-iodic water that springs naturally from the area. All 54 of the rooms and suites at Grand Hotel Terme are outfitted to promote rest and relaxation, with fine linens, soft bathrobes, and slippers rounding out the long list of amenities expected by the discerning traveler. The on-site Spa Castello, directly overlooking the lake, offers some of the most cutting edge hydro and non-hydro treatments available today, including a Jacuzzi minipool, Finnish sauna, steam bath, icefall, emotional showers, and a relaxation area. Directly accessible from the rooms by an internal lift, the Sala Relax has loungers for relaxation, an intimate lounge with fireplace, and access to the wonderful outdoor thermal pool. Cabins for beauty and thermal treatments, recommended by beauty consultants and a team of doctors, are available for guests who want to pamper themselves during their stay. Since nutrition plays a key role in achieving and maintaining a healthy lifestyle, guests may also request complete nutritional assessments and eating plans as apart of their overall wellness programs. The full service restaurant, L'Orangerie, overlooks Lake Garda and is likewise led by a chef well trained in the art and science of healthful eating that does not sacrifice taste. Local products figure prominently in the offerings, accompanied by wines chosen specifically to enhance the dining experience. Far from being a deprivational experience, a stay at Grand Hotel Terme provides plenty of time to indulge the senses and engage the mind while healing the body and soothing the spirit.

FINE POINTS

Rooms: 54 rooms.

Food: Breakfast, lunch, and dinner at L'Orangerie restaurant; also available are special nutritional programs individually crafted by top nutritionist Dr. Anna Villarini.

Special Features: All rooms are outfitted with desk, mini bar, LCD cable TV with music channels, Wi-Fi, safe, telephone, and bathrooms with bath or shower, washbasin, hairdryer, cosmetic mirror, WC, and bidet; the thermal spa centre inside the hotel offers the full spectrum of health and wellness therapies guided by top professionals in the field; bottles of Acqua di Sirmione nasal solution and an exclusive line of beauty and care products, Aquaria Thermal Cosmetics, are available for purchase; easy access to water sports, golf (guests receive a discount at nearby courses), bicycling, paragliding, and helicopter and boat tours; car rental available for trips to nearby Venice and Milan.

HOTEL CENOBIO DEI DOGI

Hotel Cenobio Dei Dogi | Via Cuneo, 34 | 16032 Camogli - Portofino Coast | Italy

Tel: +39 01857241 | Fax: +39 0185772796

E-mail: reception@cenobio.it

Website: www.cenobio.com

CENOBIO DEI DOGI grandly sits on a crest of rock above the Mediterranean Sea at the foot of Mount Portofino, just a short stroll from the old fishing village of Camogli. We're delighted to share this gem, which lies in such close proximity to the Cinque Terre, Portofino, and Santa Margherita Ligure, and is reminiscent of the time when few people knew of their magical allure. The hotel is surrounded by a lush park bordering the characteristically colored houses of the eastern Ligurian Riviera. Over four centuries ago Genoese Doges discovered this tranquil corner of what has been fittingly named "Paradise Gulf." Inspired by its peace and beauty, the Doges decided to claim this spot as their retreat, or cenobio. A 16th-century chapel dedicated to St. Emilio is still open to guests. The villa was passed down through generations of heirs, then purchased by the De Ferrari family, who in 1956 transformed it into a hotel. Antiques, Oriental rugs, and Etruscan artifacts adorn the hotel. Cenobio Dei Dogi's guest rooms and suites are simply furnished, offering either sea or garden views; we suggest one of the rooms with extensive balconies and striking vistas of Camogli's fishing port. Delight in the seawater swimming pool on the panoramic terrace with lounge-side service. Full service is also available at the private beach, which assures an uncommon luxuriousness among this popular area. Typical Ligurian dishes and seafood are featured at the Dei Dogi Restaurant, while wonderful seasonal specialties can be savored during the summer at La Playa. Cenobio's cuisine prevails on its own, but combine the exceptional food with the seaside location of both restaurants, waves pounding the shoreline, exceptional wine, and top-notch service, and the total experience reigns supreme.

FINE POINTS

Rooms: 105 rooms; 4 suites.

Food: Traditional Ligurian dishes and seafood are featured at the Dogi Restaurant, while delightful seasonal specialties can be savored in the summer at the La Playa seaside restaurant.

Special Features: Swimming pool; tennis court; paddle trips along the coastal inlets; snorkeling; diving tours guided by local experts; meters from train for independent excursions to neighboring towns of the Italian Riviera; 7 meeting rooms for groups of 10 to 200 people, many with sea view and all with natural light and modern technical equipment and services.

HOTEL CIASA SALARES

Strada Prè de Vì 31 | Loc. Armentarola, I-39036 S. Cassiano | Alta Badia, Dolomiti, Italy

Tel: +39 0471849445 | Fax: +39 0471849369

E-mail: info@ciasasalares.it

Website: www.ciasasalares.it

HOTEL CIASA SALARES is a family-run alpine retreat in the Alta Badia, literally translated as the "heart of the Dolomites." Located between lush mountain pastures and the majestic, sheer cliffs iconic to the area, the Alta Badia has been deemed a UNESCO World Heritage site for its stunning geography. Unsurprisingly, these breathtaking peaks provide world-class alpine recreation, and Hotel Ciasa Salares affords excellent access to some of Europe's best skiing and most stunning winter sightseeing. Its ski-in-ski-out location is walking distance from the Armentarola lift, which is a part of the massive Dolomiti Superski network that connects 450 ski lifts with a single pass. In the summer, the meadows are bedecked with picturesque wildflowers, and top-notch hiking, biking, and climbing for adventurers of all skill levels is available. For three generations this hotel has been run by the Wiesers, who welcome guests like family and whose knowledge of the area and passion for hospitality is contagious. The rooms are well designed with modern amenities, gorgeous woodwork, and handcrafted textiles that evoke an alpine ambiance. The excellent spa and fitness facilities offer an indoor pool, Turkish bath, Finnish sauna, and solarium. The gastronomic experience here is the cherry on top, defined by a passion for food and wine passed down through the Wieser family for generations. La Siriola features Italy's youngest Michelin-starred chef, who serves extraordinary menus celebrating excellence in cuisine in keeping with the motto "Km zero," in which ingredients are sourced according to quality, and no longer according to geographical proximity. From the five variations of foie gras, to suckling pig, to gorgeous carrot and passion fruit soup, a meal at La Siriola is an exceptional culinary adventure. Further adding to the experience is the upscale alpine décor and unique plates made from slabs of local wood, which diners may take home as a memento of their visit.

FINE POINTS

Rooms: 50 rooms.

Food: Breakfast buffet offers 140 selected products, such as fine meats, cheeses, homemade jams, freshly squeezed juices, local eggs, yogurt, mountain honey, wild salmon, homemade cakes, fresh fruit, local bread; La Terrazza offers lunch and light snacks al fresco from a traditional Laden menu; La Siriola serves innovative cuisine from five prix fixe menus as well as à la carte, with wine pairings available; on-site cheese and chocolate rooms.

Special Features: Ski-in/ski-out; spa with body treatments, massage, Turkish bath, Finnish sauna, solarium, and infrared cabin; indoor pool and fitness center; free broad band Wi-Fi throughout property; variety of children's activities plus playroom; room service; airport transportation.

HOTEL LONDRA PALACE
RELAIS & CHATEAUX

Riva degli Schiavoni | Castello 4171 | 30122 Venezia, Italy
Tel: +39 0415200533 | Fax: +39 0415225032
E-mail: info@londrapalace.com
Website: www.londrapalace.com
Skype: HotelLondraPalace

HOTEL LONDRA PALACE RELAIS & CHATEAUX is perhaps one of the most scenic hotels from which to immerse oneself in the Venetian experience. Located in the heart of the city right on the Promenade of Riva degli Schiavoni, it is just a few steps from many of the city's spectacular sites, including St. Mark's Square and Palladio's 16th-century *San Giorgio Maggiore Church*. The hotel comprises three window-filled 19th-century, five-story palazzos, whose extensive 1999 renovation was overseen by Versace boutique architect, Rocco Magnoli. The hotel's 53 rooms are all decorated in Biedermeier style, with elegant upholstery, brocades, and marble bathrooms. Each room is unique and overlooks either the lagoon or the rooftops and bell towers of the historic city center. Each space in the hotel was design to inspire and instill a sense of well being in the guests. Begin your day with the complimentary breakfast, which during the warm months you may enjoy outside on the patio fronting the promenade—the perfect spot from which to people watch. Few cities can match Venice for its combination of romance, intrigue, and history, and even one day spent investigating its myriad attractions will endear you to its charms. The hotel's location makes it easy to catch a water taxi or public boat to just about any spot in the city. Relive your memories over a superb dinner that evening at the hotel's Ristorante Do Leoni. Named after the original title of Tchaikovsky's *Symphony No. 4*, whose first three movements he wrote in room No. 106, Do Leoni serves sophisticated local and regional cuisine in an elegant room characterized by a beautiful stone-mosaic floor. A wall of windows overlooking the lagoon brings the outside in, or step out onto the waterfront terrace and cap your evening with the ultimate romantic ending—cocktails and dessert while watching the sun set over the water.

FINE POINTS

Rooms: 53 rooms.

Food: Daily complimentary breakfast buffet; dinner at Ristorante Do Lioni.

Special Features: Listed in the 2013 Condé Nast Traveler Gold List of the world's best places to stay; all rooms are non-smoking and feature satellite and SKY television, complimentary Wi-Fi, mini-bar, heating and air conditioning, safe, and turn down service; well insulated rooms with blackout curtains; some rooms with balconies; cribs and infant beds available; enjoy recreational opportunities including golfing and swimming off a scenic beach on Lido island, located a 10-minute boat ride from Piazza San Marco; boating and sailing tours can be booked from the hotel, which offers full service concierge services.

HOTEL VIS Á VIS

Via della Chiusa, 28 | 16039 Sestri Levante | Genova
Tel: +39 018542661 – 480801 | Fax: +39 0185480853
E-mail: visavis@hotelvisavis.com
Website: www.hotelvisavis.com

HOTEL VIS À VIS offers guests direct and uncompromising panoramas of the Gulf of Tigullio, from the Portofino cape to the Sestri Levante peninsula. This property offers the kind of location and views one only imagines in dreams, and it embodies the immense love of three generations bound by the extraordinary vision of Giacomo De Nicolai, the family patriarch, and his beloved wife, Flora. Giacomo spent a considerable part of his early life visiting the world's best hotels and ocean liners—at the time, one of the best ways to travel. This accumulated appreciation of the best of land and sea inspired his design for Hotel Vis à Vis as a "vessel on dry land," with vistas extending down from its prevailing hilltop location toward the Mediterranean. In keeping with the ocean liner theme, the rooms are small and basic, but each offers balcony or private garden views, with the junior suites offering the loveliest panoramas.

Two foot paths lead directly from the hotel: one traverses the old Roman road and affords magnificent sea views, while the other enables a quick descent directly into the charming fishing village of Sestri Levante and its unique shops, bakeries, cafés, and restaurants, including Hotel Vis à Vis's supreme Portobello Beach Restaurant & Bar. Overlooking the beach of the beautiful Bay of Silence, Portobello is a dreamy and romantic spot where native Chef Daniel Sanguineti's cuisine takes on a refreshing bold approach to classic Ligurian dishes. Staying true to the land, he crafts imaginative recipes artfully rich in Mediterranean flavors all perfectly paired with wines. Standouts include Sformatino di Riso all'Astice Affumicato su Zuppetta di Calamaretti al Pomodoro Fresco (smoked lobster rice flan on soup of squid with fresh tomatoes), perfectly complimented by a glass of Vermentino Colli di Luni DOC Etichetta Nera.

FINE POINTS

Rooms: 46 cabin-like rooms feature private gardens or panoramic balconies with sea, city, or hillside views; Junior Suites feature Jacuzzi bathtub and shower.

Food: Main hotel restaurant, the Olimpo overlooking the Baia del Silenzio (Bay of Silence); summertime light lunch menu at the Ponte Giunone outdoor restaurant, where they organize theme dinners and barbecues with music; Ponte Zeus panoramic terrace with bar also serves pool area; Portobello Beach Restaurant & Bar in Sestri Levante is just a short walk and is located directly on the beach of Baia del Silenzio.

Special Features: All rooms feature air-conditioning, safe, mini bar, flat screen television with digital satellite, free Wi-Fi, daily maid service, and natural products courtesy Erbario Toscano; non-smoking rooms available; activities include golfing (16 miles away), ping-pong, canoeing, hiking, cycling, free bicycle rental, diving, and snorkeling; on-site pool, sun deck; solarium, spa, massage services, hot tub, Turkish and steam baths; playground for the kids; barbecue facilities, public parking; car rental; shuttle service (surcharge); airport shuttle (surcharge); 24-hour front desk with express check-in and check-out, currency exchange, bag storage, concierge service, and tour information; lounge, television area, and family room; babysitting and child services; laundry, dry-cleaning, suit press, and ironing services; meeting and banquet facilities; fax and photocopying; newspapers; disabled guest facilities, including elevator; smoking in designated areas.

LEFAY RESORT & SPA LAGO DI GARDA

Via Feltrinelli 136 | 25084 Gargnano (BS) | Lake Garda, Italy

Tel: +39 0365241800

E-mail: res.garda@lefayresorts.com

Website: www.lefayresorts.com

LEFAY RESORT & SPA LAGO DI GARDA sits high atop the mountain overlooking Lake Garda—just one floor below heaven! The resort is a partner of the prestigious Small Luxury Hotels of the World, Healing Hotels of the World, Virtuoso, Traveller Made networks, and Mr. & Mrs. Italy Luxury Hotels. The Leali family, founders of the regional airline Air Dolomiti and renowned for their innovation, reliability, and exceptional customer care, have certainly done it again at Lefay Resort & SPA Lago di Garda. This time they have redefined luxury hospitality as beyond the realm of ostentation, opulence, and mere aesthetics, integrating ethical values such as eco-sustainability, bio-architecture, and minimum environmental impact as the key elements of this new holiday concept. The resort redefines luxury by focusing less on the material and more on the concepts of space, nature, silence, time for oneself, and discrete service that still emphasizes attention to detail.

This echoes throughout the entire property, especially through the excellence of their well chosen, highly qualified staff. The soul of the resort is the 40,000-square-foot Lefay SPA, the award-winning temple of wellness where mind and body are regenerated through rediscovery of genuine emotions and a sense of inner harmony. The cuisine is likewise exceptional. Executive Chef Matteo Maenza blends his distinct Puglian heritage and culinary flair to reflect the Lefay Vital Gourmet Concept—a modern take on the traditional Mediterranean diet using only fresh and seasonal local produce, respecting the rhythm of the seasons, and enhancing sustainability. The SPA menu emphasizes detoxifying and lower caloric ingredients to ensure energy without sacrificing the flavors and authenticity of the exquisite Mediterranean cuisine. The elaborate breakfast buffet includes a fresh juice bar with precut vegetables and fruit that are ready to blend into your own healthy creations.

FINE POINTS

Rooms: 93 suites.

Food: Daily complimentary breakfast buffet; two restaurants, La Grande Limonaia and Trattoria la Vigna; Lounge Bar; Pool Bar; room service.

Special Features: 24-hour front desk; meeting and banquet facilities; babysitting services upon request; laundry, dry cleaning, and ironing services; full service SPA facilities, including private SPA rooms and treatments that are perfect for couples; hair and beauty salon; VIP room facilities; Lefay Shop; car rental; full concierge service; golfing and variety of outdoor tours/excursions booked at front desk; airport shuttle available for extra charge.

PALAZZO VENART LUXURY HOTEL

Santa Croce 1961 | 30135 Venice, Italy

Tel: +39 0415233784

E-mail: info.venart@ldchotels.com

Website: www.palazzovenart.com/en/

PALAZZO VENART LUXURY HOTEL marries Old World Venetian elegance with modern-day services and facilities—an inviting new option for those seeking luxury accommodations in the City of Water. With a rich history dating back centuries, the Palazzo Venart (formerly the Palazzo Bacchini delle Palme) once housed some of the city's most notable figures. Completely remodeled, it is now a luxurious hotel located in the Santa Croce district alongside the Grand Canal. Many of the original features, such as the Gothic wings that now host the exhibition centre and a private home, have been retained and preserved alongside the main Palazzo complex, whose eighteen rooms and suites serve as the hotel proper. Marble stairways and historic frescoes add period charm to the corridors, rooms, and ceilings, while valuable murals capture the essence of the Palazzo's extensive history. The front entrance, accessed by private water taxi arranged by the hotel, is surrounded by beautiful gardens in which guests can relax with a drink or take in the views over the canal. Several of the Palazzo's rooms and suites also offer fabulous canal views, and all are uniquely decorated to marble bathtubs, parquet flooring, designer furniture, luxury bedding, and authentic Venetian artwork. Just off the main lobby is a private courtyard whose magnolia trees create a shaded oasis. Set within this romantic enclave is the hotel's GLAM restaurant, helmed by the award-winning—and twice Michelin-starred—contemporary Italian chef Enrico Bartolini. This intimate space is the perfect venue in which to showcase classic Venetian fare with a contemporary twist, and Bartolini and his team have certainly introduced an exciting new restaurant to the Venetian culinary scene. Dishes like risotto with porcini mushrooms and curry, spaghetti with eel and fennel, and veal sweetbreads with roasted pepper, among others, are sure to become classics. Complimented by an extensive wine list and attentive service, a meal at GLAM will be one of the highlights of your stay.

FINE POINTS

Rooms: 7 classic rooms; 4 prestige rooms; 3 luxury rooms; and 4 suites.

Food: GLAM restaurant serving breakfast, lunch, and dinner; bar/lounge; coffee bar.

Special Features: All rooms and suites feature direct-dial telephone with room service, free Wi-Fi, complimentary mineral water, wide screen satellite television, king-sized double beds or twin beds as preferred, slippers and bathrobe, ornate marble bathtubs, and mini-bars; 24-hour front desk; concierge that can arrange any number of specialized tours and activities; dry cleaning and laundry services; babysitting; airport transportation; area shuttle.

RELAIS SANT'UFFIZIO

Strada del Sant'Uffizio 1 | 14030 Cioccaro di Penango | Asti, Italy

Tel: +39 0141916292 | Fax: +39 0141916068

E-mail: info@relaissantuffizio.com

Website: www.ldcitalianhotels.com/en/hotels/relaissantuffizio/

RELAIS SANT'UFFIZIO sits amid the storybook surroundings of Monferrato in Piedmont, a region that never fails to delight with its lush rolling hills, quaint villages, and traditional vineyards. Founded in the 17th century as a monastery, the Relais Sant'Uffizio retains many of the qualities of its former incarnation as an oasis of peace and tranquility, exemplified by its elegant gardens, stately brick and columned façade, frescoed interiors, and rooms that perfectly balance style and comfort. Accommodations are available at the main house and at the monastery's former stables, the Scuderie del Sant'Uffizio, now renovated into a private and chic getaway. If rest and relaxation is on your itinerary, the experts at Aquanatura Spa will be happy to help you craft a schedule of rejuvenating treatments, from a quick massage after a long day of sightseeing to an entire stay's worth of head-to-toe pampering. You are also ideally situated to explore the cities of Asti, Turin, and Alba, as well as sites like the splendid gardens of Palazzo Borromeo a Isolabella-Stressa and the Cattedrale di Sant'Evasio, one of the finest examples of 12th century Moor-influenced architecture in Italy. Set in the heart of Italy's famous white truffle region, as well as amid numerous vineyards (including its very own), the hotel of course upholds the finest culinary standards. At the on-site restaurant, La Locanda, chef Mark Mazzocco has crafted a dynamic, seasonally changing menu that showcases the region's best known dishes made with local ingredients, including bagna càuda, a warm dip that fuses vegetables, olive oil, anchovies, and butter; vitello tonnato, cold veal with cream sauce; and bollito misto, a classic Italian stew that here is finished with shavings of the region's white truffles. Guests can also enjoy wine produced from the hotel's own estate and drinks in the restaurant bar, as well as breakfast in the Limonaia room, which overlooks the courtyard and gardens.

FINE POINTS

Rooms: 54 rooms and suites.

Food: Breakfast, lunch, and dinner served at La Locanda.

Special Features: Aquanatura spa and wellness center with wide range of massage and beauty treatments, as well as a sauna, hydro massage pool, steam bath, Mediterranean bath, ice cascade, relaxation area, and private spa for one or two people; wine tastings and tours to on-site and nearby vineyards; indoor and outdoor swimming pool; tennis courts; special wine and culinary packages; dogs allowed; free Wi-Fi.

ROMANTIK HOTEL BAITA FIORITA DI DEBORAH

Ristorante Baita Fiorita | Via Frodolfo, 3, 23030 | Santa Caterina Valfurva (SO), Italy
Tel: +39 0342925119 | Fax: +39 0342925050
E-mail: deborah@valtline.it
Website: www.compagnoni.it

ROMANTIK HOTEL BAITA FIORITA DI DEBORAH is located in the picturesque village of Santa Caterina Valfurva, right in the middle Selvio National Park at the foot of the Ortles-Cevedale mountain group in the Italian Alps. An outdoor lover's paradise, the region beckons skiers and snowshoers in the wintertime, hikers, bikers, and climbers in the warmer months. And even if your idea of adventure is nothing more taxing than a massage or a sauna at the hotel's spa, the region still has much to offer in the way of breathtaking panoramas of towering mountain peaks and lush mountain valleys teaming with a variety of flora and fauna. And the hotel is situated for easy access to it all, right in the center of town—which itself offers plenty of opportunities for leisurely scenic strolls, shopping, and people watching—while remaining an oasis of relaxation once you walk through its doors. A blend of rustic Alpine charm and the services and amenities of a top-notch hotel, it is owned and operated by the family of three-time Italian Gold Medalist and championship skier Deborah Compagnoni, who impart a genuine warmth along with their impeccable service. Accommodations include twenty-two rooms, as well as a *baita,* a traditional dwelling of the Italian Alps and Apennines that is built entirely by hand with local timber and stones, perfect for families and groups. The restaurant is also a beloved piece of history, having provided sustenance to visitors and locals alike since it was established in 1896 as Caffè Bormio. In fact, it was around this restaurant that the Compagnoni family built the hotel, and it remains a showcase of cozy elegance and exceptional cuisine. The menu focuses on traditional Italian dishes and regional specialties crafted with carefully selected, locally produced products, all served with exceptional local wines.

FINE POINTS

Rooms: 22

Food: Breakfast, lunch, and dinner at Caffè Bormio restaurant.

Special Features: Wellness center featuring sauna, Turkish bath, whirlpool, and an array of beauty and rejuvenating treatments like massage; free Wi-Fi throughout property; short walk to ski lift; access to hiking, biking, and climbing; mini-club for children offering a variety of activities, including ski lessons; shuttle bus service; airport transportation to and from hotel.

ROMANTIK HOTEL MULINO GRANDE

Hotel & Suites | Via Cisliano 26, 20090 | Cusago Milano | Italy
Tel: +39 0290390731 | Fax: +39 0287152455
E-mail: mulino-grande@romantikhotels.com
Website: www.hotelmulinogrande.it

ROMANTIK HOTEL MULINO GRANDE is a place where attention to detail is paramount, both in terms of service and ambiance. Located just west of Milan in the heart of the historic center of Cusago, the hotel is a short drive from the Rho Exhibition Center and the Cusago Castle, which can be seen from the hotel. The Mulino Grande is truly unique, due to its origins as a sixteenth-century flour mill, now masterfully renovated to reflect the principals of sustainable building and architecture, yet maintaining the integrity of the original structure. The Mulino Grande's dedication to environmental stewardship runs deep and can be observed throughout all aspects of the hotel's design and services: it is built from strictly natural materials, and its air conditioning runs off geothermal energy. Each of its twenty-one rooms boast unique designs and color schemes, all of which evoke the hotel's rustic heritage while epitomizing comfort and luxury. The hotel's eco wellness spa is also powered solely by renewable energy sources and provides a wonderfully wholesome environment in which to recharge and revitalize. True to the hotel's commitment to sustainable luxury, the Magiono Cusago restaurant and lounge specializes in "zero kilometer," seasonal dishes, with ingredients grown in the hotel's organic garden or purchased from local vendors. The carefully selected, high-quality ingredients combined with the cozy but elegant dining room make for an intimate setting in which to enjoy the local cuisine and wonderful selection of wines from all over Italy, North to South and including the islands. In the summer, enjoy a pre-dinner drink out on the terrace, which features a beautiful wrought iron patio designed by architect Antonella Tesei. In the winter, unwind by the fireplace in a warm and romantic atmosphere. Cigar lovers will be thrilled to know the lounge also offers a selection of the finest Cubans.

FINE POINTS

Rooms: 13 classic and superior rooms; 8 suites.

Food: Magiono Cusago restaurant and lounge, specializing in local and seasonal cuisine with a focus on regional dishes for lunch and dinner; free breakfast; room service.

Special Features: All rooms feature shower or tub, WC, television, telephone, air conditioning, safe, and mini bar; free WI-FI throughout rooms and hotel; wellness center features a full-service spa, Finnish sauna, Turkish bath, ice cascade, sensory showers, and relaxation room; fitness center; business center; transportation to and from airport.

ROMANTIK HOTEL REGINA

Via Passo Rolle, 154 | 38054 San Martino di Castrozza, Italy
Tel: +39 043968221 | Fax: +39 043968017
E-mail: info@hregina.it
Website: www.hregina.it

   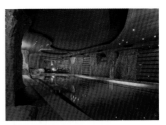

Romantik Hotel Regina is set against the magnificent Dolomites in the charming mountain town of San Martino di Castrozza in the Trentino region. Known for warmly welcoming pilgrims traveling across the Alps, the small town of San Martino established its reputation as an alpine resort and outdoor recreation destination in the late nineteenth century, due in large part to the patronage of European aristocrats and mountaineers. Situated within the Paneveggio Pale di San Martino Natural Park, the hotel is an ideal point from which to explore the priceless natural beauty of the area, as well as enjoy an abundance of outdoor activities year round. The hotel is within walking distance of the Passo Rolle slopes and nearly 40 miles of Nordic ski and snowshoe trails, and in fact caters to skiers and snowboarders, offering a private shuttle between the hotel and the mountain as well as ski, board, and boot drying and storage at the end of the day.

In the warmer months, San Martino provides a vast range of hiking, rock climbing, canyoneering, and fishing opportunities. With one of the oldest Italian hotelier families at the helm, the Hotel Regina masterfully combines alpine charm with superb elegance and hospitality. The warm hotel staff takes care to ensure that all guests enjoy outstanding service, comfort, and refined accommodations, as well as the natural beauty of the area. Its full-service spa and wellness center is the perfect place to reinvigorate after a day spent reveling in the beauty of the Dolomites. The hotel's Regina restaurant offers a memorable dining experience, whether breakfast before a day at the slopes, lunch in between scenic walks, or dinner after a full day exploring the mountains. The Regina Restaurant masterfully showcases the local cuisine, particularly the dairy and cheeses of the Trentino region, and boasts a wonderful selection of regional wines.

FINE POINTS

Rooms: 36 classic and single rooms; 7 junior suites; 4 grand junior suites; 3 top suites.

Food: Regina Restaurant and Lounge Bar, serving breakfast, lunch, and gourmet dinner; afternoon tea; and a range of European beers, local wines, and grappa.

Special Features: Wellness center featuring swimming pool, Turkish bath, indoor and outdoor Jacuzzi, cold mist, sauna, herbal tea corner, solarium and terrace, botanic garden, and fitness center with Technogym equipment; library; TV room; music room; afternoon coffee and tea; Wi-Fi throughout; guided walks; themed itineraries and trip planning consultation; night skiing; private shuttle to and from mountain during winter; free ski bus stop across from hotel.

ROMANTIK HOTEL TURM

Pizza della Chiesa 9 | 39050 Fie allo Sciliar | Alto Adige | Dolomite, Italy

Tel: +39 0471725014 | Fax: +39 0471725474

E-mail: info@hotelturm.it

Website: www.hotelturm.it

ROMANTIK HOTEL TURM is nestled amid the Italian Dolomites at the foot of the Schlern Mountains in Southern Tyrol. Melding traditional Tyrolean hospitality with international élan, it is the perfect venue for guests seeking outdoor adventure coupled with resort-style pampering. Activities abound in the nearby Schlern Nature Park, which is the site of a panoramic cableway up to the Seiser Alm, the largest high altitude Alpine meadow in Europe, and one of the region's most renowned hiking, skiing, and climbing destinations. After hitting the slopes or trails, the onsite spa is the perfect spot to relax, let go, and recharge, whether with a sauna, a swim, a workout, or some meditative time in the unique salt grotto. Treatments range from massages to hot stone to the unique "hay baths," used by local farmers for centuries to soothe and rejuvenate. The hotel itself is made up of three houses and towers. The old tower, the Turm, dates back to the 13th century, and has over the centuries served as fortification, courthouse, and jail. Back then, the area's peasants would wait for the snow to block their paths home, so they could stay at the Turm for days, playing cards, drinking, and socializing. Many things may have changed since then, but the Turm retains its historic welcoming atmosphere. Instead of a wooden bench or two, however, today's guests can choose a variety of comfortable rooms, all featuring charming regional décor, paintings from the hotel's extensive and well-regarded private art collection, and amazing views of the Schlern, especially from those at the top of the towers. The onsite Restaurant Turm has been voted one of the five best hotel restaurants in Italy, and makes for a wonderful romantic dinner, either inside the cozy dining room or outside on the terrace, surrounded by the magnificence of Mother Nature. Chef Stefan's signature style is both inventive and down-to-earth, and his dishes pair beautifully with any number of wines from the hotel's cellars.

ROYAL HOTEL SANREMO

Corso Imperatrice, 80 | 18038 Sanremo (IM), Italy
Tel: +39 01845391 | Fax: +39 0184661445
E-mail: reservations@royalhotelsanremo.com
Website: www.royalhotelsanremo.com

ROYAL HOTEL SANREMO is located on what is known as the Italian Riviera of Flowers, just south of the chic resort towns of Monte-Carlo, Nice, Cannes, and the French Riviera and only minutes from the center of Sanremo with its exclusive boutiques and famous casino. Every guest is cordially welcomed upon arrival, most by name, for they return time and again. Truly an elite, time-honored resort, the hotel is surrounded by a luxuriant subtropical park of 16,000 square meters and a heated (27°C/82°F) seawater swimming pool offering impressive cascading views over the Mediterranean. Each of the uniquely decorated guestrooms feature plush furnishings and the finest amenities. Many also offer breathtaking views, with the penthouse deluxe junior suite in particular offering stunning vistas over the sea. Free entrance to the sandy beach, sun beds, umbrellas, and cabins are available to guests at a lido opposite the hotel. The state-of-the-art Royal Wellness spa features high-end treatments like Payot Paris and Decléor, massage, a wet zone, plus fitness room and hair stylist. The Bar delle Rose is elegantly decorated, providing a cozy place to relax with an afternoon tea, espresso, light fare, or a before-dinner aperitif. Whether poolside at Corallina Bar and Restaurant, at Ristorante Fiori di Murano with its panoramic views and precious glass flower chandeliers, on the terrace at Il Giardino for a refined candlelit dinner and views overlooking the sea, or in the garden at the exclusive Capriccio Gourmet restaurant, dining here is an enchanting experience, distinguished by five-star services and a passion to generate unsurpassed Mediterranean and international cuisine. After dinner, cigar aficionados are certain to appreciate the elegant smoking lounge. Once the home of European royalty and aristocracy, the Royal Hotel Sanremo still remains the perfect place to stay between Monte-Carlo and Portofino.

FINE POINTS

Rooms: 126 rooms and suites.

Food: Fiori di Murano, Il Giardino, Corallina pool bar and restaurant, Bar delle Rose, and Capriccio Gourmet. Breakfast overlooking the sea and park at Sala Aranci or on the terrace.

Special Features: Royal Wellness spa with high-end treatments like Payot Paris and Decléor, massage, wet zone, plus fitness room and hair stylist; heated sea water swimming pool; tennis court; mini-golf; elegant smoking lounge; children's playroom and playgrounds; "Smile Club" for children with attendant in high season; baby-sitting on request; convention and banqueting facilities; free Wi-Fi; private parking and garage; transfers; car rental; 24-hour service; offsite excursion booking available; laundry and dry cleaning; water sports nearby; 18-hole golf course 5 km from hotel offering a reduction on green fees.

SINA CENTURION PALACE

Dorsoduro 173, 30124 | Venezia, Italy
Tel: +39 04134281 | Fax: +39 0412413119
E-mail: centurionpalace@sinahotels.com
Website: www.centurionpalacevenezia.com

SINA CENTURION PALACE is a place where the ancient magic of Venice comes together perfectly with the essence of modern style and luxury. Situated on the Grand Canal, but also away from throngs of tourists, the Hotel Centurion is set in Venice's Dorsoduro neighborhood, home to a vibrant population of artists, writers, designers, and students. Located between the renowned Peggy Guggenheim modern art museum and the famed Basilica Santa Maria della Salute, and close to the iconic Gallerie dell'Accademia, Hotel Centurion grants amazing access to the very best of Venice's celebrated art culture. A renovated Venetian palazzo with high ceilings and arched doorways, the hotel is characterized by its essential Venetian-Gothic architecture infused with a contemporary, boutique feel. The Centurion's rooms and suites exemplify 21st–century Italian opulence, with their splashes of vibrant color and chic furnishings and accessories. At the same time, the palpable romance of Venice is undeniable, thanks to incredible views of the city. Dining al fresco is an exhilarating experience, as the on-site Michelin-rated Antinoo's Lounge and Restaurant is situated right on the Grand Canal, its bustling comings and goings serving as a romantic backdrop to a fine selection of authentic and gourmet Venetian cuisine, complete with a wine list offering the best from many different regions of the country. The intimate hotel bar is likewise another perfect place to take in this enchanting city, a cocktail or flute of Prosecco in hand, as the sparkle of sunlight against the water gives way to the twinkle of evening candlelight.

FINE POINTS

Rooms: 50 rooms, including two dual-level suites.

Food: Antinoo's Lounge and Restaurant, serving breakfast, lunch, and dinner.

Special Features: Private water taxi dock to receive guests; pet friendly (dogs allowed); meeting rooms; free Wi-Fi; fitness center; 24-hour room service; butler service; multi-lingual staff; concierge; tour-booking; laundry, dry cleaning, and ironing; babysitting; 24-hour front desk.

VILLA CORDEVIGO WINE RELAIS

Località Cordevigo | 37010 Cavaion Veronese (VR), Italy

Tel: +39 0457235287 | Fax: +39 0456268482

E-mail: info@villacordevigo.com

Website: www.villacordevigo.it

VILLA CORDEVIGO WINE RELAIS was built in the 18th-century as a residence for local nobility. An ambitious restoration project brought the villa back to life for modern times, where it once again serves as an elegant refuge for visitors who wish to immerse themselves in the romance of the Italian countryside. Situated amid the vineyards and olive groves typical of the Veneto region, the property exemplifies its owners' deep respect for nature and the proper management and use of its bounty. The region of Cordevigo literally means "vitality of the heart," implying a place where the whole of nature is alive and transmitting a positive energy. The age-old cypresses, oaks, flowerbeds, and greenery that comprise the exterior landscape are carefully tended to enchant the guests as well as honor the rhythms of the seasons. Years of history, culture, and respect for the land are also woven into the neat rows of vines belonging to Vigneti Villabella, a winery founded in 1971 by Walter Delibori and Giorgio Cristoforetti. Inside, every effort has been made to preserve the magnificent furnishings, decorations, and artwork that have been housed inside these walls for centuries. The spacious rooms and suites likewise retain their historic ambiance, furnished with fine fabrics and finishes that include wooden beamed ceilings, marble bathrooms, and terra cotta floors. The mix of classical elements with contemporary luxuries results in accommodations that are as sophisticated as they are charming. The same attention to detail is showcased at the hotel's Oseleta restaurant, which was awarded the coveted Michelin star in 2013 based on executive chef Giuseppe D'Aquino's sublime orchestration of various culinary elements into a symphonic whole. Dinner is the best time to sample not only various dishes of the region, but also its wines, including those made on the premises from Bardolino Classico and Cavaion Veronese grapes.

FINE POINTS

Rooms: 27 rooms and 7 suites.

Food: Free buffet breakfast and a la carte lunch and dinner at Oseleta restaurant.

Special Features: Luxury full-service spa with beauty and wellness treatments, sauna, steam bath, and sensory showers; tea and relaxation area; fitness center; outdoor swimming pool; bicycle rentals; free Wi-Fi throughout; conference space and meeting areas; 24-hour front desk; concierge; ticket and tour bookings; car service; dry cleaning and laundry; special packages.

VILLA PRINCIPE LEOPOLDO & SPA

Via Montalbano 5 | 6900 Lugano, Switzerland (Ticino, Italy)

Tel: +41 (0) 91 985 88 55 | Fax: +41 (0) 91 985 88 25

E-mail: info@leopoldohotel.com

Website: www.leopoldohotel.com

VILLA PRINCIPE LEOPOLDO & SPA is located in Ticino, an Italian-speaking region of southern Switzerland known for its lakes and the Mediterranean flavor of its architecture and cuisine. This five-star property sits on Lake Lugano, famous for its crystal clear waters and picturesque, garden-dotted waterfront promenade. Lugano itself is a blend of upscale chic and old-world charm, as renowned for the neoclassical buildings that line Piazza della Reforma as it is for its luxury shopping along Via Nassa in the city's center. The town is also a favorite destination for lovers of the great outdoors, as funiculars transport hikers, and campers to the nearby mountain. A former residence of the Hohenzollern noble family, who ruled Prussia and then Germany for 170 years, the villa maintains its rich sense of history even as it caters to discerning modern travelers, including a number of celebrities.

Chief among its charms are 37 beautifully decorated and comfortable suites that range in size from 500 to 1,350 square feet, luxury treatments offered at the Kiso SPA and wellness center, a fitness area, and an expansive terrace that overlooks Lugano Gulf. Another terrace, the Limonaia, is a sunny spot from which guests can enjoy breakfast in the warm-weather months, surrounded by fragrant lemon trees and views of the grounds. The matchless excellence of the hotel's culinary fare reflects the exceptional talent and experience of award-winning chef de cuisine Daria Ranza and his two sommeliers-maitres d'hotel, Claudio Recchia and Gabriele Speziale. Together, they showcase modern and classical dishes with Mediterranean influences, accompanied by a wide selection of renowned wines and spirits, including the signature offering of the hotel's own vineyard, the Rosso del Principe.

FINE POINTS

Rooms: 37 suites.

Food: Restaurant serving breakfast, lunch, and dinner; piano bar and lounge.

Special Features: Full service boutique SPA and wellness center, featuring exclusive beauty treatments along with a Jacuzzi, sauna, and Turkish bath; fitness center with qualified personal trainer leading Pilates, yoga, and Fit Walking classes; outdoor swimming pool; two open-air tennis courts; bicycle, electric bikes, and Maserati rentals; wine-tasting events; free Wi-Fi.

VILLA & PALAZZO AMINTA
HOTEL BEAUTY & SPA

Via Sempione Nord | 123 28838 Stresa (Verbania) Italy
Tel: +39 0323933818 | Fax: +39 0323933955
E-mail: info@villa-aminta.it
Website: www.villa-aminta.it

VILLA & PALAZZO AMINTA HOTEL BEAUTY & SPA is a peaceful haven facing Lake Maggiore between the towns of Stresa and Baveno and overlooking the Borromeo Gulf and islands. Once a private residence, the nineteenth-century property has been transformed into a five-star luxury hotel by the Zanetta family, the owners since 2000. They have brought the villa back to its original splendor, combining a fairy tale feel with elegance, taste, and the highest standards of amenities and service. The only hotel on Lake Maggiore that has been designated a "Leading Hotel of the World," the property is lavishly decorated with antique furniture, stuccos, frescoes, Murano chandeliers, precious wallpapers, arabesques, and Oriental arches. The romantic hotel guestrooms range from midsize to spacious, each one tastefully and comfortably adorned. All open onto balconies or terraces with garden or lake views. We are partial to the suites, with their wonderful lake front balcony views, all personalized and located on the top fourth floor. The luxurious Palazzo Aminta Beauty & Spa offers exclusive programs to rebalance the body and soul. Escape into their Zen meditation room for the deepest level of relaxation or indulge in a host of other healthful and beautifying services. Leisure activities abound, including special boat excursions leaving from the hotel docks for an unforgettable visit to the Borromeo Islands. Along with all their fine service and amenities, Villa & Palazzo Aminta also contains two wonderful restaurants. Ristoranti Le Isole serves an extensive breakfast buffet, lunch, and dinner in a beautiful dining room offering panoramic lake views, which can be enjoyed al fresco during the warmer months. As one of the top restaurants in the region, Ristoranti I Mori is especially noted for its wine list, carefully chosen for discerning palates. But the real wow factor there is native-born executive chef Giuseppe Vigna, who utilizes only the best Piedmont ingredients to deliver imaginative cuisine rooted in his family's heritage and treasured recipes.

FINE POINTS

Rooms: 53 deluxe rooms; 13 suites; 6 junior suites.

Food: Restaurant Le Isole with a 4-course menu and restaurant I Mori with à la carte menu.

Special Features: Special events and ceremonies; meeting room to accommodate from 10 to 100 persons; multilingual reception and concierge; outdoor swimming pool; private beach; 3 boat moorings; limousine and helicopter services; private shuttle to and from Stresa; 24-hour room service; baggage and garage service; water skiing; parachute; jet ski; natural park; Palazzo Aminta Beauty & Spa, offering treatments designed for new mothers, four-handed massage with essential hot oils, seaweed therapies or thermal mud bath, exfoliating, hydrating and revitalizing face and body treatments, and more; fitness area; cooking lessons; cocktail-making lessons; wine tasting.

Piacenza

Gazzola

Parma

Reggio Emilia • Modena

Ferrara

Emilia-Romagna ◉ Bologna

Ravenna

Forlì

Cesena

Rimini

Montegridolfo

Pesaro

Carrara
Massa
Forte dei Marmi
Pietrasanta
Pistoia
Prato
Vicchio di Mugello
Settignano
Florence ◉ *Candeli*
Bagno a Ripoli

Lucca

Pisa

Livorno

Barberino Val d'Elsa

Colle Val d'Elsa

S. Giustino Valdarno

Arezzo

Tuscany

Siena

Cortona

Urbino

Marche

Ancona

Macerata

Fermo

Marina di
Castagneto

S. Giovanni
d'Asso

Valiano

Montepulciano

Lago Trasimeno

◉ Perugia

Spello

Ascoli Piceno

Isola di Capraia

Campiglia Marittima

Poggi del Sasso

Umbria

Elba

Castiglione della Pescaia

Grosseto

Saturnia

Lago di Bolsena

Spoleto

Teramo

Pescara

Terni

Viterbo

Rieti

◉ L'aquila

Chieti

Lago di Bracciano

Lazio

Abruzzi

Nerola

Vatican City ★ *Rome*

Grottaferrata

Frosinone

Latina

Central Italy

Central Italy is the country's geographic and cultural heart, embodying all the qualities we would consider quintessentially Italian. Certainly, a tour of this region is a must on any Italian travel itinerary, whether that includes Tuscany's sun-drenched vineyards, olive groves, and charming villages, Marche's lively coastal towns, Umbria's historic Etruscan sites, or the magnificent art cities of Florence, Rome, Pisa, and Siena. Hidden treasures off the beaten path abound as well, rewarding the intrepid traveler with an ever-expanding appreciation for this abundant land. Your culinary adventures will be enlightening. Tuscany is of course famous as a gourmand's paradise, as is Emilia-Romagna and Umbria, home to some of the world's great cheeses and pastas. Marche and Abruzzo offer outstanding seafood, and Lazio provides distinctively unique local wines.

Emilia-Romagna

Known for its cuisine, diversity of landscapes, and a wealth of historic towns, this region attracts visitors seeking a variety of amusements. The coastal towns of Rimini and Misano Adriatico are a summer paradise with miles of sandy beaches. Just about any outdoor activity is readily available from these locations, including deep-sea fishing, hot springs, mud baths, and water sports. Additionally, these towns boast a wealth of restaurants and nightclubs. The charming city of Ravenna, capital of the Western Roman Empire in the 5th and 6th centuries, is situated on the Adriatic coast halfway between Venice and Florence, and is best known for the brilliant mosaic ornamentation of its Byzantine churches and tombs. On the banks of the river Po is the superb Renaissance city of Ferrara with its palazzos (palaces), shops, cafés, and narrow medieval streets. In San Marino, cars are forbidden, which facilitates the exploration of this marvelous medieval city by foot. There is much to discover when wandering along winding narrow streets lined with red-roofed stone houses, medieval walls, and fortresses. Bologna is not only the capital and heart of Emilia-Romagna, it is also home to notable Renaissance artists Carracci and Parmigianini and opera's incomparable tenor, Luciano Pavarotti.

At Gran Meliá Rome Villa Agrippina, Chef Alfonso Iaccarino's cuisine showcases the finest of the region's flavors, products, and culinary traditions. His belief that what we eat is a critical factor in health and wellbeing translates into a dedication to sourcing the best local and seasonal produce.

Lamborghini and Ferrari sports cars and Ducati motorcycles are manufactured here. Cobbled streets provide pathways to the city's Romanesque and Gothic architecture, as well as medieval palazzos and majestic towers.

Classic Cuisine: Emilia-Romagna is politically considered a single region, but is in fact two, especially with respect to cuisine. Emilia, the region's capital, is north of Bologna. Romagna is located to the south. As such, Bologna embodies distinct characteristics of both Emilia and Romagna. The foods of both areas are hearty and feature the three main cooking fats of butter, oil, and lard. Bologna la grassa (Bologna the Fat) is a title the city has acquired for its characteristically rich cuisine, the quality of its pork products, and the richness of its pastas. Tagliatelle and lasagna are favorites, but tortellini is one of its most renowned dishes, served stuffed with Parmesan cheese, pork, raw ham, turkey breast, egg, and mortadella (minced pork meat). Emilia, specifically Parma, is the home of salamis. It is thought that Parma's prosciutto (cured ham) is sweeter than that of any other region in Italy. Culatello di Zibello (cured leg of an adult hog) is another specialty. Modena features the Zampone and Cotechino di Modena, which are cured meat products made from a combination of pork taken from striated muscle fibers, pork fat, pigskin, and different seasonings. Romagna's food preparation on the other hand embraces aromatic herbs and the use of skewers to roast seafood, chicken, game, other meats, and a variety of sausages. Vegetables are simply but flavorfully prepared in dishes such as asparagi alla parmigianna (baked asparagus) or melanzane marinate (marinated eggplants). Emilia-Romagna has two other great culinary contributions: balsamic vinegar, which has been made in Modena for centuries, and Parmigiano Reggiano, the unsurpassed king of cheese, made in the provinces of Parma, Reggio, and Emilia for over seven hundred years.

Classic Wines: The vast majority of wine produced in this region is not DOC level, and the Lambrusco has produced a sea of poor-quality sparkling wines that have tarnished the region's reputation even further. But there are producers trying diligently to break through the stigma. Albana di Romagna is Italy's first white DOCG. While its quality can vary, the passito (a generic term meaning made from dried grapes) wines show promise. Colli Bolognesi Classico Pignoletto is the area's second DOCG, producing dry, crisp whites made from the Pignoletto grape. Cletto Chiarli produces some stunning wines as well. Their "premium" bottling is the perfect food wine. A visit to this picturesque winery, with its Old World charm and unmatched hospitality, is the perfect day trip. You will find this area very visitor friendly, dotted with many other wineries at which you can enjoy lunch or tastings. The region also produces some good international varieties. Tenuta Palazza's Magnificat Cabernet Sauvignon is top notch. A great way to get a thorough overview of this massive region's offerings is to visit Enoteca Regionale Emilia-Romagna in Dozza. Here, you can sample most of the wines produced in the region—and in the basement of a medieval castle to boot.

Classic Pairings: Lambrusco is the perfect match for Prosciutto di Parma, but can also exquisitely compliment a Parmesan-stuffed tortellini. The wines are incredibly versatile in their ability to complement food.

Tuscany

Tuscany, Toscana in Italian, is the most well-known Italian region, and is distinguished by many small, picturesque hilltop towns. Most are situated on gently rolling hillsides amid vineyards and olive groves, winding roads, ancient villas, and castles. Florence, Pisa, Lucca, and Siena are the region's most well-known cities, and together they offer visitors many fascinating attractions. Florence is of course the renowned home of history's greatest artistic geniuses: Leonardo da Vinci, Michelangelo Buonarroti, and Filippo Brunelleschi. Their work, as well as that of many other generations of artists up to the present time, is

featured in the scores of museums and public places scattered throughout the city. The Uffizi, the most select picture gallery in the world, displays Renaissance art featuring the works of da Vinci, Botticelli, Michelangelo, Raphael, Canaletto, and many more. Visit the Rooms of the Planets at the Galleria Palatina. The Galleria dell'Accademia hosts very important collections of paintings along with well-known works by Michelangelo, including Il Gigante, more commonly known as the Statue of David. The collection at Stibbert's museum focuses on the history and traditions of various cultures, and includes weapons, armor, costumes, furnishings, and examples of the applied arts in the form of 16th- to 19th-century tapestries and paintings. Visit the Medici Chapel and the Buonarroti House, both of which contain sculptures by Michelangelo. The Museo degli Argenti, or Silver Museum, is located in Palazzo Pitti and houses various precious objects such as gems, cameos, semi-precious stones, ivories, jewels, and silver. In Pisa, the Leaning Tower is of course the main attraction. Lucca, the birthplace of Giacomo Puccini, is a charming walled city, and Siena, with its Piazza del Campo, is home to the world-famous Palio horse race. Venturing outside these munic-

ipalities will put you in the heart of some of the most authentic medieval villages and seaside towns: southeast of Florence, one finds Arezzo, Cortona, Montepulciano, and Montalcino; south of Florence and Siena is San Gimignano, Pienza, Pitigliano, Saturnia, Grosseto, and the island of Elba; northwest of Florence are located Lucca, Pisa, Forte dei Marmi, Pietrasanta, Viareggio, and Carrara.

Classic Cuisine: When you think of Italian cuisine, the highly publicized Tuscany most certainly comes to mind. Its approach to food has always been one of simplicity, founded on a love of wine, olive oil, and bread. Leftover bread is never wasted but used as the main ingredient for several common dishes. Most well known are Panzanella salad made with bread, tomato, onion, and olive oil, and Ribollita, a thick soup prepared with green vegetables, cabbage, beans, bread, and olive oil. Fresh pasta, particularly parppardella, ravioli, pici, and tordelli made with chestnuts, Pecorino cheese (usually sheep or goat), beans, prosciutto, basil, rosemary, marjoram, bay leaves, sage, parsley, and thyme, has been part of the Etruscan kitchen for centuries. Vegetables combined with fish, beans, and meats grilled over an open fire are regular fare on the Tuscan table. One such dish is bistecca alla Fiorentina, a thickly cut steak seasoned only with olive oil, salt, and pepper. Many Tuscan dishes center around vegetables such as artichokes, asparagus, fennel, peas, spinach, and mushrooms. Besides steak, Tuscan meat dishes include wild game and boar, duck, rabbit, and beef tripe. Although you will find dishes like sogliola alla Florentine (sole) on inland menus, coastal Tuscan cuisine incorporates a wider variety of fish, as demonstrated in recipes such as sarde in marinara (marinated sardines), Triglie alla livornese (red mullet), and cacciucco all livornese (fish stew made in the Tuscan port of Livorno). Tuscany is known for several different desserts, but none are more famous than the simply delicious biscotti (hard cookie), made exclusively for dipping in sweet Vin Santo or espresso.

Classic Wines: When picturing Italy, images of Tuscany's rolling hills covered in vines and olive trees come to mind. Tuscany has had a long history of wine fame. Medieval Florentine poet Dante Alighieri was famously noted for his written praise of the Vernaccia grape, which hailed from San Gimignano. Yet many Americans will remember when Tuscan wines were considered something of

a joke—every table in every so-called Italian restaurant throughout the U.S. would feature a straw-covered bottle of bland red wine, ironically named "fiasco." Since then, however, winemakers have been removing mass producing vines in favor of smaller quality plantings. Sangiovese, the red grape of Tuscany, is responsible for most of the region's great wines. Although the Chianti DOCG has been expanded fairly dramatically, the Classico region still produces top notch Chianti. Look for the black rooster signifying the Classico designation. Brunello di Montalcino produces big, bold expressions of Sangiovese that can age for decades. Vino Nobile di Montepulciano DOCG is also a Sangiovese-based wine that is slightly more delicate, and it pairs well with lighter pasta dishes. Bolgheri produces great international varietals. As the only white DOCG in Tuscany, Vernaccia di San Gimignano produces crisp, fruity whites from the Vernaccia grape. Vin Santo, which means holy wine, lives up to its name. It's a high-alcohol dessert wine produced from Trebbiano and Malvasia grapes whose vines were traditionally hung vertically from the towers of the estate, allowing the wind to blow through and dry out the grapes. Modern producers use circulation fans

that achieve the same results. The result is a sweet, honey- and almond-flavored amber liquid that is indeed heavenly.

Classic Pairings: Bistecca alla Fiorentina is traditionally matched with a Chianti Classico and is a must try.

Marche

This region lies on the eastern side of central Italy, between the Adriatic Sea and the Apennine Mountains. Many travelers who come to the Marche are looking for the "authentic" Italy, untarnished by crowds, but welcoming of outsiders. The hilltops are strewn with scenic towns and castles, some lending magnificent views all the way to the sea. The Marche is typically known for its seaside beach resorts, the larger of which are now quite bustling and known for their lively, upbeat nightlife. Some main locations include Gabicce Mare, Pesaro, Fano, San Benedetto del Tronto, and Senigallia, famous for its "Velvet Beach." Monte Conero, however, with its white limestone cliffs and rocky coves, is unlike anything else along this section of Adriatic coastline. Here, the primary towns are Urbino, an important city for visitors interested

in fine Italian art and architecture; Ancona, with its busy seaport and main ferry connection to Croatia, Greece, and Turkey; and Macerata, famous for its annual outdoor opera festival. Pesaro is an appealing seaside resort known for its furniture production, beaches, shops, and—as Rossini's birthplace—home of the Rossini Opera Festival and a conservatory founded with a legacy from the composer. Ascoli Piceno is southern Marche's epicenter, and its Renaissance-style main square, *Piazza del Popolo* ("Square of the People"), is considered one of the most beautiful in Italy. Long-established records indicate Ascoli Piceno was home to more than two hundred towers in the Middle Ages. Today, about fifty still exist.

Classic Cuisine: Pasta dishes reign supreme, particularly tagliatelle with a vegetable, fish, or meat sugo (sauce); vincisgrassi, rich baked lasagna with ground pork, mushrooms, and tomato and béchamel sauce, topped with truffles; and passatelli, strands of pasta made from breadcrumbs, Parmesan cheese, and egg cooked in broth. Mountain-cured ham and grigliata mista di carne (charcoal-grilled meat) are highly popular as well. Favorite meats include veal, rabbit, quail, pigeon, chicken, and goose, which are often cooked in a porchetta style like coniglio in porchetta (stuffed rabbit with fennel, garlic, and rosemary). Along the coast, fresh seafood is traditionally served, especially brodetto, a fish stew made with thirteen different varieties of fish. Funghi (mushroom), nuts, herbs, game, tartufi bianco (white truffles), and tartufo nero pregiato (black truffles) are widely used in the Marche. Pecorino di San Leo, a sheep's milk cheese, is exceptional, as is Casciotta d'Urbino, a crumbly, semi-cooked cheese made from a blend of whole sheep's milk and whole cow's milk.

Classic Wines: There are several DOCGs in Marche. Two of

the most highly regarded are Matelica Riserva and Castelli di Jesi Verdicchio Riserva. They produce nuanced, age-worthy versions of the Verdicchio grape. Conerro Rosso Riserva DOCG produces reds from the Montepulciano grape, and a smaller percentage of Sangiovese. It's often aged in new French oak barrels and shows intense character.

Classic Pairings: The Verdicchio grape's great crisp nature lends itself to pastas as a vibrant contrast.

Umbria

Located in the middle of Italy, Umbria is the only region in the central part of the country without a coastline. Umbria is often referred to as the "green heart of Italy," with its medieval towns and characteristic lush, green rolling hills. The prominent towns include Orvieto, with its magnificent Gothic duomo (cathedral) and glittering façade; Spoleto, home of the Festival dei Due Mondi (Festival of Two Worlds), a worldwide attraction that includes music, dance, and theatre scenes; and Assisi, the birthplace of St. Francis. Perugia is the region's capital and a very important Etruscan city, whose stunning architecture includes the Etruscan Arch and the Etruscan Well. Top museums include Perugia's National Gallery, with the largest collection of Umbrian art in the world and a comprehensive collection of Perugian paintings. Imaginative palaces, monasteries, and churches enhance the region's distinctive hillside towns of Gubbio, Spoleto, Todi, Spello, Città di Castello, and more. Many of these architectural gems are also known for fine handmade ceramics and savory black truffles. Umbria is home to Lake Trasimeno, where you can take a jaunt by boat to one of its many islands with their beautiful beaches.

Classic Cuisine: Umbria's food consists of some basic ingredients: premium olive oil, Durum wheat pasta, hog, lamb, and colombaccio (pigeon). Two specialties of the region are mazzafegati, sausages made from hog's liver, pine nuts, orange peel, raisins, and sugar, as well as tartufo nero (black truffles), grown beneath the earth and served over everything including Pecorino cheese. Due to their limited quantities, these truffles are one of the most expensive foods in the world. Many variations of homemade egg pasta, notably tagliatelle, ciriole, and stringozzi, are prepared in a decadent black truffle sauce unique to the region. Umbria is also responsible for the production of much of the dried pasta consumed throughout Italy. Umbrians cook a wide range of foods that incorporate fish, meat, game, vegetables, and rice, as well as a variety of herbs and spices. A classic menu may include frittata ai funghi (mushroom omelet), minestra di riso (rice soup with lentils), and pollo alla cacciatore (chicken with capers and olives).

Classic Wines: The most renowned wine of this region is Orvieto, a crisp, light white made from Grechetto and Trebbiano Toscano grapes—which also produce the majority of the wine in the region as a whole. One of the highest quality reds is Sagrantino di Montefalco DOCG. Sagrantino is a highly tannic grape that is also high in alcohol. It is a stubborn little fruit that demands patience: it should be aged a minimum of three years prior to release. It takes even longer to come into its own, but it's worth the wait.

Classic Pairings: Sagrantino is difficult to pair with food because of its strength. However, mazzafegati, or wild boar, has an assertive enough flavor profile that the wine and food complement each other without a power struggle.

Lazio

The cradle of Roman civilization, Lazio is home to its greatest manifestation, the Eternal City. Most certainly, Rome is not to be missed during one's travels to central Italy. Principal sights of interest include Vatican City and its museums that house Raphael's rooms; the Sistine Chapel; the Basilica of St. Peter and

St. Peter's square; Villa Borghese; the Colosseum; the Roman Forum; Piazza Navona; Piazza Farnese; the Pantheon; the Jewish Ghetto; Trastevere; and the outdoor market at Campo de' Fiori. Also, put aside some time for exploring the exclusive shops along the Via Veneto and around the Spanish Steps. According to tradition, throwing a coin into the Trevi Fountain ensures you will return to the Eternal City. Around Rome, also visit: Tivoli, best known for Villa d'Este with its unique gardens, gravitational water system, and fountains; Frascati and Grottaferrata, located in the Castelli Romani hills overlooking the city of Rome, which have been a favorite summer retreat of the Romans since antiquity; Ostia Antica, the old Roman port with some of the oldest remains in Lazio; Lake Bracciano, the eighth-largest lake in Italy, with its medieval village of Trevignano, many lakeside cafes, and restaurants; and the Orsini Odescalchi castle dating from the 12th century. Water sports are popular in this area as well. Noteworthy Etruscan cities worth visiting are Cerveteri, Tarquinia, and Viterbo. Visit the Tyrrenian Sea at Civitavecchia,

especially in summer, when you can relax on sandy beaches and snorkel the reefs that are common along its coastline.

Classic Cuisine: The traditional food of Rome and Lazio has always made abundant use of fresh, seasonal produce grown throughout the countryside: artichokes in spring, mushrooms in autumn, and luscious figs and watermelon in the summer months. Many Roman dishes are well seasoned with onions, garlic, rosemary, sage, and bay leaves. Pasta takes on its own character in Roman specialties, like *Bucatini all'amatriciana* with tomatoes and a spicy bacon sauce, *Fettuccine alla Romana*, linguini with a chicken liver sauce, and *penne all'arrabbiata* with a spicy chili pepper sauce. Meat dishes include *saltimbocca alla romana* (veal cutlets with sage) and *abbacchio alla Romana* (braised lamb with a garlic sauce). *Carciofi* (artichokes) are well regarded and may be prepared in one of two ways: *alla giudia* (Jewish style) or *alla Romana* (Roman style), cooked in oil with garlic and parsley. Possibly the most familiar Roman specialty is *Bruschetta*, toasted bread rubbed with a clove of garlic then drizzled with olive oil and salt, or chopped fresh tomatoes. Pecorino, a flavorful sheep's milk cheese, is often incorporated into dishes, while a mild Ricotta is used as a filling for pizzas and as an ingredient in the Roman dessert *torta di ricotta*.

Classic Wines: This populated region encompasses Rome, which is one of the major consumers of the white wines of Lazio. Malvasia and Trebbiano Toscano are the majority of wine produced. Surprisingly, red accounts for less than a quarter of production. Frascati Superiore and Cannellino di Frascati were awarded DOCG in 2011. Some of the best wines produced are from the Falco Estate, but they are from international varieties such as Cabernet Sauvignon and Merlot. Est! Est!! Est!!! di Montefiascone, a Trebbiano-based blend noted for its colorful origin story, is the most well-known wine in Lazio. It was apparently discovered when a traveling bishop charged his aide with finding the best wine in the region. Upon finding it, the aide wrote "here it is!"—"est!"—three times on the door of the inn where the wine was served. We don't know where that inn is today, but grab a bottle and sit in front of the Trevi Fountain instead. It may provide clarity and peace.

Classic Pairings: The light bodied whites made from Trebbiano are lovely accompaniments for the traditional bruschetta of the region.

Abruzzo

This region, together with Molise, forms the "ankle" of Italy. It hugs the southeastern seaboard with expansive sandy beaches extending from the north along the Adriatic, directly southward to Pescara. Traveling west from the sea, this region becomes dominated by the Apennines Mountains. Abruzzo is usually thought of as being out-of-the-way and isolated, marked only by desolate hill towns clinging to the sides of mountains. Abruzzo, along with some of the other southern regions, epitomizes a way of life impervious to change for centuries. Here, you will find a land of shepherds, uncultivated countryside, and desolate castles. Sulmona, an active town with about twenty-five thousand residents, sits four hundred meters above sea level in the center

of Abruzzo. It has narrow streets, tree-lined *piazzas* (squares) with imposing houses, especially along Via dell'Ospedale, and displays fine architecture festooned with carved windows and remnants of frescos and sculptures. You will find shops selling blankets, shawls, and sweaters, all made with local wool by the women of Sulmona, whose handiwork is legendary. To the east of Sulmona are the sixty-one peaks and heavily wooded valleys of Maiella National Park, offering climbing, skiing, walking, and bird watching. Abruzzo National Park, with its fertile landscape, towering peaks, rivers, lakes, and woodlands, is one of the most important in all of Europe. It provides refuge for more than forty species of mammals, thirty kinds of reptiles, and three hundred species of birds, including the white-backed woodpecker and golden eagle. Along with opportunities for paddling, horseback riding, and skiing, a widespread array of trails provides hikers of all levels of experience with miles of exploration.

Classic Cuisine: The food in Abruzzo is memorable. Their cuisine is highly flavored, mainly with *pepperoncini* (hot red peppers), olive oil, wine, garlic, rosemary, and aromatic saffron, which is considered to be the most symbolic ingredient of Abruzzo's time-honored cuisine. Mushrooms are integrated into almost everything. Shepherding remains the daily way to make a living; therefore, lamb, kid, sheep, and mountain goat are the primary meats served roasted or grilled. Many people still raise their own pigs, which produce tasty, lean meat and flavorsome *salami*. In seaport areas, a variety of fresh fish is incorporated into savory soups. Pasta is most often the first course and *maccheroni alla chitarra* (guitar pasta) is the most typical, wherein sheets of egg dough are cut with a flat rolling pin on a wooden box with strings. Pecorino d'Abruzzo, the local sheep's cheese, and Burrata, spheres of a luscious Mozzarella-like cheese with a soft buttery center, are specialties of this region. *Scrippelle*, or crêpes, are traditionally served as dessert, but in Abruzzo, they are rolled with tasty fillings, placed into broths, or served with cheese, vegetables, and meat.

Classic Wines: Montepulciano d'Abruzzo Colline Teramane is the region's only DOCG. The wine is made with the Montepulciano grape. The two most quality-minded producers are Edoardo Valentini and Emidio Pepe.

Classic Pairings: Montepulciano d'Abruzzo is a rustic and soft red wine with a slightly tannic finish. It is highly aromatic, with pepper, spice, and earthy notes. When pairing it with the spicy, aromatic dishes of the region, it is possible to achieve peace in the chaos of flavors.

A. ROMA LIFESTYLE HOTEL

Via Giorgio Zoega, 59 | 00164 Rome, Italy
Tel: +39 0687800168 | Fax: +39 0687811813
E-mail: info@hotel-aroma.com
Website: www.ldcitalianhotels.com/en/hotels/a-roma/

A. ROMA LIFESTYLE HOTEL is a versatile, upscale hotel in a peaceful neighborhood with convenient access to Rome's city center. Just a 20-minute drive from the airport, the hotel is perfect for those in transit, though also serves as an excellent home base from which to explore the city. A. Roma is walking distance from main bus and train lines for guests who prefer to find their own way around, yet also offers a shuttle bus service that takes guests to the heart of Rome. With extensive conference and meeting facilities and high speed Wi-Fi throughout the building and grounds, this hotel caters to the modern traveler who mixes business and pleasure. Regardless of business amenities, the stylish interior, beautiful suites, and attentive staff make this property ideal for anyone seeking an impeccable luxury experience in Rome. Its impressive selection of spacious and well-appointed rooms and suites are archetypes of comfort and class. In keeping with the spirit of elegance, the vast spa and wellness center evokes the splendor of Ancient Roman baths. In addition to the Finnish sauna, Turkish bath, bio sauna, and indoor pool and relaxation area, a wealth of revitalizing body, facial, and beauty treatments are also available. Another indulgence is the restaurant Sapori dal Mondo, which features an extensive and delicious buffet that provides a truly diverse, global approach to the dining experience. The open kitchen allows for guests to marvel at the talent of the chefs as they prepare meals inspired by cuisines from all over the world, while the hotel's romantic Rooftop Sky Stars bar is the perfect location to take in the panoramic views of Rome while enjoying a glass of wine or a cocktail. Two additional bar options provide similarly convivial experiences: Il Giardino, the lively terrace bar; and the Pool Bar, where relaxation and comfort are paramount.

FINE POINTS

Rooms: 276 rooms, including 4 different styles of suites.

Food: Daily breakfast, lunch, and dinner buffets at Sapori dal Mondo; 3 bars; room service.

Special Features: Extensive wellness center and spa with Finnish sauna and bio sauna, Turkish bath, indoor spa pool, Roman impluvium, panoramic relaxation area, body treatments, and massage; butler service; shuttle bus into the city center; free Wi-Fi throughout the building and grounds; state-of-the-art conference facilities; wedding planning services; babysitting; airport transportation.

ALDROVANDI VILLA BORGHESE

Via Ulisse Aldrovandi, 15 | 00197 Roma, Italy

Tel: +39 063223993 | Fax: +39 063221435

E-mail: Hotel@aldrovandi.com, reservations@aldrovandi.com

Website: www.aldrovandi.com

ALDROVANDI VILLA BORGHESE is the epitome of sophistication and elegance in one of the most upscale areas of Rome. Located at the edge of the Borghese gardens in the posh residential neighborhood of Pinciano, this hotel is wonderfully removed from the crowds of the city yet is a short walk from its most famous attractions, including the Spanish Steps, Via Veneto, the Galleria Borghese, and the National Gallery of Modern Art. Nestled within a lush private garden, this 19th-century villa is accented with marble surfaces and lavish chandeliers and hosts a gracious and impeccably attentive staff. In addition to a gorgeous outdoor pool lined with palm trees and verdant hedgerows, Aldrovandi features a full-service La Mer Spa with a range of beauty and body treatments, as well as a modern fitness center. Furthermore, the hotel's proximity to the extensive Borghese Gardens provides a lovely, convenient venue for walking and jogging. The Assaje restaurant is the hotel's culinary crown jewel, serving authentic, contemporary Italian cuisine indoors in an elegant setting in the colder months and outdoors in a lovely private garden throughout the spring and summer. The extensive wine cellar is stocked with some of the best of Italy's viticulture, and the knowledgeable staff is happy to assist with pairings. The magnificent breakfast spread is another opportunity to revel in the esteemed gastronomy of this hotel, while the Garden Bar overlooking the pool serves a variety of light menu items, from salads to smoothies, throughout the summer. Traditional Roman dishes for lunch and dinner are served year-round in the intimate and relaxed atmosphere of the Grill, and the American Bar, open throughout the year, proffers cocktails in a sleek setting.

FINE POINTS

Rooms: 103 rooms, including 19 suites.

Food: Breakfast, lunch and dinner at Assaje restaurant; relaxed lunch and dinner at the Grill; light fare at the Garden Bar near the pool; cocktails, beer, and wine at the American Bar; 24-hour room service.

Special Features: La Mer Spa with body and beauty treatments; state-of-the-art fitness center; outdoor heated pool; large private garden; concierge; meetings rooms; complimentary valet parking and car service to and from the Spanish Steps and Via Veneto; complimentary bike rental; transfer to and from airport or train station; complimentary use of computers and iPads; free Wi-Fi; babysitters available.

ANTONELLO COLONNA RESORT & SPA

Via valle fredda 52 00030 | Labìco – Roma

Tel: +39 069510032

E-mail: resort@antonellocolonna.it

Website: www.antonellocolonna.it

ANTONELLO COLONNA RESORT & SPA is a one-of-a-kind boutique hotel set in a historic region just outside of Rome, deep in the heart of the Castelli Romani. Situated inside the natural park of Labico, the resort is located in the middle of a conglomeration of towns and villages, once a summertime destination of Roman nobles. The resort is the creation of owner Antonello Colonna, a Michelin-starred chef whose family has been influential in the local culinary community since the 19th century. Located on a working farm on an expansive estate within a large nature preserve, the resort feels far removed from the clamor of city life but is under an hour by car from the center of Rome. Amid so much natural beauty, and with hiking, horseback riding, and food markets nearby, this property is the perfect location for visitors to experience the wonders of rural Italian life. Governed by a markedly modern, minimalist aesthetic, and with just 12 rooms, a stay here is intimate and exclusive. The accommodations are stylish, bright, and comfortable, with excellent views of the surrounding area. Ancient springs that date back to the time of Roman emperors are the inspiration for the resort's spa, which offers a range of detoxifying services and treatments involving local, natural products. Colonna's menu changes seasonally and showcases the finest products and flavors of the area. The cuisine is based on historic fare traditional to the region, but is infused with creativity and adapted to a contemporary palate. A curated collection of the area's best wines adds another dimension of locality to the cuisine.

FINE POINTS

Rooms: 12 rooms.

Food: Antonello Colonna restaurant serves traditional local dinner fare with a modern twist in a sophisticated setting. Breakfast served daily with homemade cake, jam, and other fresh products.

Special Features: Outdoor pool; on-site garden; spa with indoor heated pool, Finnish sauna, Turkish bath, frigidarium, emotional showers with aroma and color therapy, hammam massage, body treatments, and relaxation room with fireplace; 50-acre nature preserve; annual cultural program covering art, architecture, photography, design, and fashion; event space; multimedia conference room; free Wi-Fi; complimentary parking; dog friendly; airport transportation.

AUGUSTUS HOTEL & RESORT

Viale Morin 169 - 55042 | Forte dei Marmi, Italy
Tel: +39 0584787200 | Fax: +39 0584787102
E-mail: info@augustus-hotel.it
Website: www.augustus-hotel.it/en/

AUGUSTUS HOTEL & RESORT is situated along one of the most spectacular sections of Forte dei Marmi, a favorite destination for travelers who want to enjoy the region's renowned social, cultural, and recreational options. Nestled on the shore in the shadow of the nearby Apuan Alps, the hotel offers unique access to both pristine pine forests and stretches of white sandy beaches. Several types of accommodations are available, but the star of the resort is Villa Agnelli, the former seaside home for more than thirty years of the Angelli family, who founded Fiat and eventually made this resort town into a fashionable destination for wealthy northern Italian industrialists and businessmen. The villa sits within a park-like setting, surrounded by shaded gardens bursting with greenery. An alleyway of hydrangeas leads to a private underpass, ensuring exclusive access to the beach while avoiding the street. Sun and swim enthusiasts rave about the hotel's private beach, featuring over 100 tents and a heated saltwater pool and Jacuzzi. An additional heated outdoor pool is located at the main resort, as is a full-service day spa. Those wishing to stay fit while vacationing can take a yoga class on the beach, work out at the on-site fitness center, run or walk along the beach, or bike or hike in the nearby mountains. Cultural opportunities abound as well, and include art exhibitions in nearby Pietrasanta, boutique shopping in the town's center, fine dining and nightlife along the seafront, and visits to the Perini yatcht-building operations and the marble quarries used by Michelangelo. Lunch or dinner at Bambaissa Beach Restaurant, with its veranda overlooking the sea, is a romantic spot for intimate candlelight dinners or festive gatherings. Chef Gianluca Grosso offers a creative cuisine that is based on fish and that revisits Italian food with sophisticated combinations of flavors. The rich choices at lunch, the intriguing evening menu, and the extensive wine list all meet the taste of the most discerning palates.

Rooms: 19 rooms in Villa Agnelli, along with a 1,300-square-foot apartment with independent entry and 4 connecting rooms. Other accommodations include 26 rooms at the main resort, Villa Pesenti; 23 rooms at La Nave ("the ship," for the way the building's shape mimics the prow of an ocean liner); and 7 private garden villas.

Food: 3 full-service restaurants, 2 bars, beachside snacks and drinks, free breakfast. Special children's menus.

Special Features: Day SPA and fitness center; private gardens with wide variety of blooming flowers in spring and summer; heated outdoor pool at the main villa and at the beach; private beach with tents, deck chairs, pool, Jacuzzi, and food service; fleet of sailing and rowing boats available for short trips on the sea; sailing courses; bicycle rental; variety of trips booked at concierge include mountain and road biking, tennis, wine and farm tours, sailing or motor boating excursions, private airplane trips, and transfer services for Florence, Pisa, Lucca, Siena, and the Tuscan Maremma with private cars or helicopters; children's swim lessons available in the summer; babysitting upon request; free parking; pets allowed.

FINE POINTS

BORGO SCOPETO RELAIS

Strada Comunale 14 | Siena Vagliagli, 18 | Località Borgo Scopeto | 53019 Vagliagli (SI)
Tel: +39 0577320001 | Fax: +39 0577320555
E-mail: info@borgoscopetorelais.it
Website: www.borgoscopetorelais.it

BORGO SCOPETO RELAIS is a refurbished Tuscan villa perched at the top of a hill just outside the city of Siena. Travelers seeking an immersive experience in the famed Tuscan lifestyle will certainly find it here, as the property's distinctive stone buildings and grounds are faithfully preserved, it's olive groves and vineyards meticulously cultivated. Surrounded by pristine countryside, this little corner of paradise overlooks the city of Siena and the surrounding Chianti hills, which make for particularly luminous views during sunrise and sunset. Borgo Scopeto has 58 elegant rooms, all individually decorated in a chic international style while still remaining respectful of the building's original seventeenth- and eighteenth-century structures and materials. Some rooms feature an independent entrance and overlook the gardens—a great choice in spring and summer. Others rooms overlook the countryside or the charming village just down the road. There is also a separate one-bedroom apartment that is perfect for guests up to five people. The Borgo is especially popular with guests who love the great outdoors. Enjoy a round of laps in the sparkling outdoor swimming pool, play an energetic round of tennis, rent bicycles for a jaunt down into the village, or spend the day exploring the nearby hiking trails on foot. If you're up for even more adventure, rent one of the Vespas available to guests and motor into Siena to explore one of the world's great art cities. Soothe any sore muscles at the on-site spa, whose treatments include regular and hot stone massages, body wraps and scrubs, and aromatherapies. An olive oil producer for centuries, the estate even has its own cosmetics line featuring natural products like oil, wine, and honey. Lovers of Italian wine and gastronomy can enjoy tastings of the property's vintages and olive oils, and enjoy those ingredients in the culinary creations at La Tinaia restaurant, located in the old cellars of the Borgo and decorated in the typical Sienese style of the premises.

FINE POINTS

Rooms: 58 rooms and suites, one villa apartment.

Food: Complimentary breakfast every morning from 7:30–10:30 a.m. La Tinaia restaurant serving regional specialties and local wines. Bar and lounge. Poolside bar.

Special Features: Air-conditioned rooms and public areas; free Wi-Fi in rooms and throughout property; full service SPA and fitness center with Turkish bath, Hammam, and hot tub; two swimming pools; tennis courts and hiking/biking trails nearby; bicycle, Vespa, and vintage sports car rentals; wine and olive oil tastings; shopping at the famous "Mall" fashion outlet in Incisa Valdarno is an hour away by car; other tours booked at concierge; free parking.

CASTEL MONASTERO

Loc. Monastero d'Ombrone 19 | Castelnuovo Berardenga | Siena, 53019, Italy

Tel: +39 0577570570 | Fax: +39 0577570868

E-mail: reservations@castelmonastero.com

Website: www.castelmonastero.com/en/home

CASTEL MONASTERO has a long and storied history that begins in the 11th century, with its construction as a monastery in the secluded and peaceful Chianti hills above Siena. It has since served as a castle, a residence for a series of noble families, and then as part of a romantic hamlet. In its current incarnation as a luxury resort, Castel Monastero epitomizes the kind of immersive experience visitors expect from a sojourn in Tuscany: the ability to experience firsthand the heritage of the land and the people who have made fine living a high art. Passing through the courtyard of the estate, surrounded by the massive stone-wall and tile-roof buildings so distinctive to the region, you might feel as if you've been transported back in time. Every window in the individual rooms and suites opens onto a charming series of bucolic vistas, from sweeping vineyards to lush woods to verdant fields. While it's clear from the sophisticated furnishings and accessories of the interiors that you are in the modern era, they are nonetheless influenced by the rich colors and textures of the surrounding countryside. If daily jaunts in the great outdoors don't recharge your batteries, the on-site spa and wellness center boasts a broad range of state-of-the-art detoxification, rebalancing, and reshaping therapies. Obviously, culture, emotion, and memory are all part of the Tuscan experience, and its cuisine and wines are no exception. Experience the best of both in the resort's exemplary restaurants, Contrada and La Cantina, which are under the direction of executive chef Stylianos Sakalis and culinary personality Gordon Ramsay, who boasts a collection of ten *Michelin* stars along with an absolute passion for Tuscany. Together, the two men have crafted menus showcasing the eternal masterpieces of Italian cuisine using only the finest ingredients native to the region.

CASTELLO DEL NERO HOTEL & SPA

Strada Spicciano, 7 | 50028 Tavarnelle Val di Pesa | Florence | Italy

Tel: +39 055806470 | Fax: +39 05580647777

E-mail: info@castellodelnero.com

Website: www.castellodelnero.com

CASTELLO DEL NERO HOTEL & SPA, an authentic twelfth-century castle located in the heart of the Chianti wine region in Tuscany, is a luxury hotel offering the latest in modern facilities while maintaining the elegance and glamour of its Old World past. Surrounded by 740 acres of rolling Tuscan hills dotted with vineyards and olive groves, the hotel is perfect for guests seeking a break from the hustle and bustle, a romantic sojourn with a loved one, an exploration of the region's food and wine, or a base from which to explore the cities of Florence, Sienna, and Pisa. A member of the Leading Hotels of the World, Castello del Nero is the first luxury hotel in the Chianti region to offer an exclusive destination SPA, designed by global spa specialist ESPA. Amid a relaxing atmosphere defined by elegant woods, smooth glass, and cool stones, guests experience the very best in holistic treatments and services, including signature treatments and body rubs using extra virgin olive oil prepared from olives grown and harvested in the estate,

sea salts, essential oils, and other healing ingredients. Under the strict supervision of the Italian Fine Art Commission, the hotel's rooms and suites have been painstakingly restored to uncover a priceless collection of art treasures and original features. Located in both the main castle building and in the charming farmhouse annexes facing the castle, the rooms and suites are individually decorated in various period style while offering the kinds of amenities appreciated by discerning travelers. Amid the refined elegance of this superb property is one more reason to immerse yourself in its beauty: Michelin-starred La Torre restaurant. Not only does executive chef Giovanni Luca di Pirro utilize herbs grown from the castle's garden and oil from the property's olive trees, he also partners with the producers of the best Tuscan products available. The chef also supervises La Taverna restaurant, with its authentic Tuscan cuisine. La Taverna moves out by the pool in the summer, offering magnificent views of the private estate.

Rooms: 32 double rooms and 18 suites.

Food: Buffet breakfast and gourmet dining at La Torre restaurant; buffet breakfast and dinner on the garden terrace in good weather; drinks at The Bar; Tuscan dishes and informal dining at La Taverna or La Taverna by the pool.

Special Features: In-room amenities include air-conditioning, telephone, LCD television with complimentary channels on demand, free Wi-Fi, safe and mini bar, desk and chairs, large closets, showers and tubs; meeting room with video conferencing and equipment; on-site private chapel; on-site ESPA-designed SPA featuring the very best in holistic treatments and services; spacious air-conditioned Fitness Suite with TechnoGym machines and equipment and views of the surrounding hills; nearby trails for running, hiking, and biking; outdoor swimming pool; tennis courts; concierge services, including tour bookings; wine and extra virgin olive oil tastings at the on-site wine cellar available by arrangement; courtesy shuttle to/from Florence or Siena according to schedule.

CASTELLO DI TORNANO

Loc. Tornano | 53013 Gaiole in Chianti | Siena, Italy
Tel: +39 0577746067 | Fax: +39 0577746094
E-mail: info@castelloditornano.it
Website: en.castelloditornano.it

CASTELLO DI TORNANO bears the weight of centuries of fascinating history, from its establishment as a fortified medieval castle within a wooded hamlet to its modern-day incarnation as a picturesque hotel and winery. The property has belonged to the Selvolini family of Florence since the 1970s, and their masterful renovations have transformed the castle into a model of hospitality within the Chianti region. While the full tales of the myriad rivalries and plots, loves and losses, joys and sorrows that have played themselves out within these stone walls are lost to the mists of time, today's guests will no doubt add their own stories to the intricate tapestry of this history. Set amid the gently rolling Chianti hills, dotted with vineyards and olive groves, the hamlet offers visitors an unparalleled Tuscan experience. The castle's accommodations include ten elegant double rooms and suites located in the castle tower, one double room with a private patio, as well as seven cozy country-style apartments away from the main building, each with their own entrance, living room, kitchenette, bathroom with shower, and private outdoor space with table and chairs. The property's ancient barn has been transformed into a charming two-bedroom, 750-square-foot cottage with two bedrooms and private Jacuzzi. All accommodations include large flat-screen televisions and central heating. And while apartment and cottage guests have the option of cooking in their kitchens, a visit to the on-site restaurant at least once is a must. Here, the chef creates traditional Chianti dishes using only the freshest locally sourced ingredients, including seasonal vegetables from the kitchen's garden, the property's very own IGP Tuscan extra virgin olive oil, local cold meats and cheeses, and game like pheasant and wild boar, hunted on the property's grounds. The Selvolinis also run the on-site winery, which showcases the Sangiovese grape in a variety of wines to enjoy at dinner as well as sample and purchase at the local wine shop.

FINE POINTS

Rooms: 10 rooms inside castle (2 suites, 2 triple, 6 double); 1 double room with private patio; 2 apartments with 1 double room; 5 apartments with 2 bedrooms; and 1 two-bedroom cottage.

Food: Breakfast, lunch, and dinner; wine shop open March through November, every day from 9:00 a.m. to 8:00 p.m.

Special Features: Swimming pool built in what was once the castle's moat; tennis courts and ping pong tables; walking, hiking, and bicycling all available from the hotel; cooking classes and wine tastings; free unlimited Wi-Fi throughout property; Golf Club Ugolino a Grassina, one of the most scenic courses in Italy, is only a 45-minute drive away; Siena is 20 minutes away by car.

DUOMO HOTEL

Via Giordano Bruno | 28 47900 Rimini, Italy

Tel: +39 054124215/6 | Fax: +39 054127842

E-mail: info@duomohotel.com

Website: www.duomohotel.com

DUOMO HOTEL is the inaugural hotel project from internationally renowned architect and designer Ron Arad. This exciting modern concept, with its bold colors, sleek textures, and futuristic shapes, is unlike any other hotel in the city. From the entrance through doors outfitted with oversized pinball flippers for knobs to the giant stainless steel ring that serves as the reception desk to the space-age room interiors, every element is a showcase of modern Italian design that marries functionality with innovative shapes and just a bit of humor. Accommodations include two sizes of rooms (with shower only, and with larger bathrooms that include jetted tubs), as well as nine "DreaMing" suites that range in size from 375 to 450 square feet, and come with private courtyard, king-sized bed, and Jacuzzis. All rooms and suites feature flat-screen televisions, satellite channels, pay TV, Sky Vision Gold, cordless phones with voice mail, high-speed Internet access, and light dimmers. Located on a quiet street in the center of Rimini, the DuoMo is the perfect spot from which to explore the town and the nearby beach, which is a short ride by bicycle or a 15-minute walk. Nearby streets are dotted with chic cafes, restaurants, and shops, and the town's wealth of historical attractions are all within short walks or cab rides. Not to be missed is the nearby beach and marina, the Tiberius Bridge, the Arch of Augustus, and the medieval Sismondo Castle, the location for important local art exhibitions as well as weekly markets. The hotel is famous for its extensive breakfast buffet, served every morning from 7:00 a.m. to 11:00 a.m., as well as for its cocktails and social scene at NoMi bar. There is no lunch or dinner service, but the front desk is happy to recommend nearby venues to match any taste and dietary requirement.

FINE POINTS

Rooms: 43 rooms and 9 DreaMing suites.

Food: Extensive daily breakfast buffet with fresh fruit and variety of breads, juices, and coffee drinks; beer, wine, and cocktails at on-site NoMi bar; front desk is happy to recommend nearby restaurants for lunch and dinner.

Special Features: Massages and body treatments available in-room or inside the hotel's mediation room through a partnership with Swiss Dermolab, a leader in the wellness industry; bicycles available to cycle to the beach; every level features and "honesty bar," where guests take what they want and write it down; free Wi-Fi throughout hotel; the new Palcongressi event center is a little over a mile away by foot; golf club 12 minutes from hotel; 40 minutes away by car to Ravenna; 10 minutes by taxi to the train station.

THE FIRST LUXURY ART HOTEL ROMA

Via del Vantaggio, 14 | 00186 Roma
Tel: +39 0645617070 | Fax: +39 0645617079
E-mail: info@thefirsthotel.com
Website: www.thefirsthotel.com

THE FIRST LUXURY ART HOTEL ROMA is a former nineteenth-century nobleman's palace that has been transformed into one of the most elegant five-star hotels in Rome. Trendy yet warm and inviting, it has been conceived as a new concept in hospitality. More than just a place to stay, it is also a cultural experience, offering guests the best in contemporary and traditional Italian furnishings, art, and cuisine. Located in the historic heart of the city, the hotel is minutes from the dozens of sites that make Rome one of the world's most popular travel destinations. Once inside, however, the hustle and bustle of the outside world gives way to an enveloping atmosphere of refined relaxation, exemplified by the stunning showcase of designer furnishings and artwork by some of the most important contemporary Italian artisans. This art gallery feel extends to the rooms and suites, all of which are likewise outfitted with chic furnishings and unique artworks, along with luxury bedding and a host of thoughtful amenities. And while most urban hotels only offer glimpses of their cities from windows and small balconies, First Luxury Art Hotel Roma puts the entire city in your line of sight from their magnificent rooftop terrace. With its near-wrap-around views, and fabulous food and drink, the terrace is rapidly becoming one of the places to see and be seen during the warm weather months. For an unexpected pleasure, indulge in the creations of the hotel's signature restaurant and be surprised by the breathtaking views from the exclusive Rooftop Garden. Those seeking the best in contemporary Italian cuisine will delight in a menu that puts an innovative spin on traditional dishes, while feeling right at home thanks to attentive service and an atmosphere that is both modern and welcoming.

FINE POINTS

Rooms: 23 suites and 6 classic double rooms.

Food: Rooftop terrace service for lunch and dinner, weather permitting; breakfast, lunch, and dinner; beer, wine, cocktails, and bar menu at the Lounge Bar.

Special Features: All rooms and suites are 100 percent non-smoking and feature contemporary design details, furnishings, and artworks; Sky television available in all rooms and suites; check-in available directly from room, with welcoming glass of champagne; free Wi-Fi in rooms and throughout the entire hotel; full-service concierge to assist with a host of needs, from booking tickets to planning itineraries; multi-lingual interpreter available 24/7; Birò electric car available for rental; private car service; access to nearby fitness center; babysitting available with advanced notice; on-site personal shopper and art consultant; laundry and shoe shining; business center; five minutes by foot to the metro station; twelve minutes by car to Termini Train Station; fifty minutes by car to Fiumicino Leonardo Da Vinci airport.

GRAN MELIÁ ROME VILLA AGRIPPINA

Via del Gianicolo, 3 | Rome 00165, Italy
Tel: +39 06925901 | Fax: +39 0692590300
E-mail: gran.melia.rome@melia.com
Website: www.melia.com/en/hotels/italy/rome/gran-melia-rome/index.html

GRAN MELIÁ ROME VILLA AGRIPPINA is a luxury resort experience in the heart of Rome. Situated on the banks of the Tiber, this urban oasis is just a short stroll from the most iconic Roman sites, including the Vatican, Piazza Navona, Campo dei Fiori, and the Pantheon, yet the expansive gardens insulate the hotel from the hustle and bustle of Rome's cultural epicenter that lies just outside its doors. Notably, the Villa Agrippina houses several ancient archaeological relics, including the ruins of the original villa, once home to the mother of infamous Roman Emperor Nero. The distinctly Roman-inspired architecture melds seamlessly with a contemporary chic, creating an air of ageless grandeur. The accommodations are irrefutably elegant, featuring high ceilings, large windows, sumptuously draped fabrics, wooden floors, modern art, gorgeous bathrooms, and a personal espresso machine in every room. Some rooms feature private gardens, while others have their own terrace complete with outdoor whirlpool overlooking the Vatican and Castel Sant'Angelo. Amid immaculately kept foliage, a beautiful outdoor pool and lounge area offer an excellent locale from which to relax. Finally, some of the best Mediterranean cuisine in the entire city is available at Viva Voce, the hotel's sophisticated restaurant that serves a creative yet authentic menu sure to impress even the most discerning palate. Chef Alfonso Iaccarino's cuisine showcases the finest of the region's flavors, products, and culinary traditions, and his belief that what we eat is a critical factor in health and wellbeing translates into a dedication to sourcing the best local and seasonal produce.

FINE POINTS

Rooms: 116 rooms and suites.

Food: Gourmet dining at Viva Voce; casual dining at the Nectar Bar, an elegant venue serving breakfast, lunch, and dinner; afternoon tea and a champagne and martini bar at the Library, a stylish and peaceful fireside salon with views of the Vatican walls; poolside snacks, light lunch, and cocktails at Liquid Garden and Bar.

Special Features: Spa my Blend by Clarins, offering beauty treatments and services, massage, private Turkish bath, external vitality pool, relaxation lounge area, steam room with chromo and aromatherapy, sauna and gym; free Wi-Fi throughout hotel; three meeting rooms with natural daylight equipped with modern audiovisual equipment; shuttle bus service to the Ara Pacis; babysitting on request; dry cleaning and laundry services; parking available.

GRAND HOTEL CONTINENTAL

Via Banchi di Sopra, 85 | 53100 Siena, Italy

Tel: +39 057756011 | Fax: +39 05775601555

E-mail: reservation.continental@royaldemeure.com

Website: www.grandhotelcontinentalsiena.com

GRAND HOTEL CONTINENTAL is a former seventeenth-century palazzo that has been meticulously refurbished into a boutique hotel that retains the opulence of its Renaissance heritage. As the only five-star hotel in the heart of Siena, it is a monument to the city's storied past and an epitome of modern luxury run by friendly, impeccably trained staff. The building is an architectural jewel, commissioned by Pope Alexander VII as a wedding gift for his niece. The interiors impart a refined and romantic atmosphere, with grand frescos, priceless furniture, and polished marble defining the hotel's common spaces, the most unique of which is the beautiful ballroom, or *Salone delle Feste*, perfect for private functions and celebrations. Each of the rooms and suites are likewise havens of comfort and elegance, with additional frescoes, historic paintings, inlaid silver

mirrors, Chinese porcelain lamps, and priceless silk draperies. Centrally located within the city's old walls, the hotel is an easy walk to a host of shops, restaurants, and attractions, including the cathedral and Piazza del Campo. The concierge excels in planning itineraries, so don't be shy about engaging their expertise. And if part of your stay includes indulging in the best of Tuscan food and wine, you can enjoy both without ever leaving the hotel. Its Ristorante Sapordivino, helmed by noted chef Luca Ciaffarafà, offers a selection of exquisitely revisited Tuscan dishes matched with some of Italy's most important vintages from the on-site wine cellar, which is carved into the base of the medieval tower. Meals may be enjoyed in the elegant Sala Gori or outside in the inner courtyard, with its glass cupola and refined atmosphere.

FINE POINTS

Rooms: 39 rooms, 12 suites.

Food: Breakfast, lunch, and dinner, as well as fine wines, beer, and cocktails, at Ristorante SaporDivino; room service.

Special Features: All rooms feature individually controlled summer air conditioning and winter heating, minibars, safes, flat screen LCD and satellite televisions, direct-dial phones, hair dryers, and courtesy toiletry kits; Wi-Fi throughout the hotel; laundry, dry cleaning, and ironing service available upon request; meeting and banquet facilities; the Salone delle Feste grand ballroom is available for a private functions; variety of special packages available, including one that focuses on the art and culture of Siena; nearby parking garage; 24-hour front desk with multi-lingual staff; concierge services; baggage storage.

GRAND HOTEL DE LA MINERVE

Piazza della Minerva, 69 (Centro Storico) | 00186 | Roma, Italia

Tel: +39 06695201 | Fax: +39 066794165

E-mail: reservations@ghminerve.com

Websites: www.grandhoteldelaminerve.com

www.minervaroofgarden.it

GRAND HOTEL DE LA MINERVE is a standout among Rome's five-star luxury hotels, a refurbished six-story seventeenth-century palace that retains the noble elegance of its original architecture. How pleasing to find such a warm and welcoming hotel in the center of Rome—luxurious in its appointments but boutique in size. It is run with such seamless precision that you're left alone to relax, but if you get within fifty feet of the front door, the concierge is on the spot, inquiring about your wishes, ready to call a cab or hand you an umbrella should you choose to stroll the Eternal City. Its central location, just off the Piazza della Minerva that is also home to Bernini's famous elephant and obelisk, makes it the perfect spot from which make your explorations. The magnificent reception area with its stained glass ceiling and plush sofas and chairs is a welcoming oasis from the bustling streets, and all 119 rooms and 17 suites are outfitted for comfort and convenience. Some even have small balconies, and the higher story rooms provide great views of the city, including the Pantheon, which is just across from the hotel. During the summer months, the bar is open to the Minerva Roof Garden, while the restaurant is open on the Roof Garden all year long. Here you can enjoy delicious Italian and international cuisines while soaking in spectacular views—it will seem like you can nearly reach out and touch the Pantheon. And while Rome's nightlife is legendary, make sure to rise early at least once for breakfast at La Cesta. Open daily from 6:30 a.m. to 10:30 p.m., it offers a wonderful breakfast buffet with hot and cold beverages, bacon, eggs, and sausage, an array of delicious pastries, and an abundance of fresh fruit. The cuisine at lunch and dinner is fundamentally Roman, yet innovative to the point of being stimulating to the eyes and palate.

FINE POINTS

Rooms: 123 rooms and 12 suites.

Food: Minerva Roof Garden restaurant, serving Italian and International cuisine for lunch and dinner; La Cesta restaurant, serving breakfast; Le Cupole bar, serving an array of beer, wine, and spirits; room service.

Special Features: All rooms feature marble bathrooms with Etro bath amenities, double glazed windows, flat screen televisions, telephones, movies on demand, safes, and mini-bars; additional amenities, like a welcome gift and Bulgari toiletries, are included with the four suites, each named for notable former residents, the writers Stendhal, Herman Melville, George Sand, and Count Vittorio Alfieri; also on site is a fitness room, and there is free Wi-Fi throughout property; transfers to and from the airport can be arranged for a fee.

GRAND HOTEL PRINCIPE DI PIEMONTE

Piazza Puccini, I - 55049 | Viareggio (Lu), Italy

Tel: +39 05844011 | Fax: +39 058440180

E-mail: info@principedipiemonte.com

Website: www.principedipiemonte.com

GRAND HOTEL PRINCIPE DI PIEMONTE is an elegant coastal getaway in the Tuscan beach town of Viareggio. Originally constructed in the 1920s, this hotel earned a name for itself as the destination of internationally recognized artists, celebrities, aristocrats, and intellectuals, and its splendid façade has served as the backdrop for numerous cinematic productions. Situated on the beach just a short drive from Pisa—and walking distance from the boutiques, jewelers, restaurants, cafes, and nightlife of Viareggio—this hotel is the perfect location to experience the Italian Riviera at its finest. Each of the hotel's five floors embody a different style of decor, ranging from 18th-century Paris to Art Deco. The rooms are splendidly designed, with marble bathrooms, hardwood floors, and French doors that open onto balconies overlooking the Apuan Alps or the Tyrrhenian sea. A picturesque rooftop pool with comfortable day beds is the ideal spot from which to take in the views and sip cocktails in the sun, while the beach just outside the hotel welcomes guests with all necessary amenities, including a heated pool with sea views, open year round. The spa has a range of beauty and massage services, as well as a fitness center, saunas, steam room, and spa-jet. The Piccolo Principe is the hotel's culinary crown jewel and recipient of two Michelin stars, serving traditional flavors and dishes of the area, and the land and sea tasting menus showcase the freshest seafood, meat, and produce. Open May to October, it offers seating inside an elegant dining room, as well as outside on the lovely rooftop terrace. The wine cellar has a fabulous selection from Tuscan producers both large and small, with other excellent Italian and foreign wines available.

FINE POINTS

Rooms: 106 rooms.

Food: Complimentary breakfast daily; dinner at Piccolo Principe and rooftop from May to October; lunch and dinner year round at Regina Restaurant; beer, wine, and cocktails available at Regina's wine bar, at the pool bar, on the terrace, or in the lobby salon; room service.

Special Features: Spa with range of beauty and body treatments, sauna, Turkish bath, steam room, and relaxation area; fitness center; business center with meeting rooms and conference facilities; wedding services; free Wi-Fi throughout hotel; dry cleaning; currency exchange; garage parking.

HOTEL BRUNELLESCHI FIRENZE

Piazza Santa Elisabetta, 3 | Firenze 50122

Tel: +39 05527370 | Fax: +39 055219653

E-mail: info@hotelbrunelleschi.it

Website: www.brunelleschihotelflorence.com

HOTEL BRUNELLESCHI FIRENZE is a four-star boutique hotel located in the historic city center of Florence. Once owned by Renaissance architect Filippo Brunelleschi, the property includes Pagliazza Tower, which is the oldest structure in Florence, and San Michele in Palchetto Church, which serves as the hotel's entrance and reception. The result of renowned architect Benelli's careful renovations, the buildings have been re-orchestrated into an enchanting set of lodgings that epitomize classic Florentine design. The rooms are especially charming, with their oak floors, tall ceilings, and luxurious beds outfitted with velvet headboards and canopies made from fine fabrics woven exclusively for the hotel. For a special treat, book the pool suite, with its Jacuzzi and amazing views of Giotto's bell tower and the cathedral; or the deluxe executive, from which you can enjoy equally breathtaking panoramas right from bed.

The color theme of plum (the color of Florence), light green, and dove grey ties everything together into a harmonious and romantic whole. Indeed, romance is always in the air here, in every sense of the word—the hotel was even mentioned in the finale of Dan Brown's book *The Da Vinci Code*. Few properties in the city allow guests to so easily immerse themselves in the Florentine experience, and you're only a short walk from the Dome, the Piazza della Signoria, the Uffizi, and the amazing shopping along Ponte Vecchio. Once back home from your adventures, relax with a drink at the Florence Tower Bar, and then choose from among two restaurants that excel in the ambiance and flavors that have made Florence a destination for foodies from around the world: the Osteria della Pagliazza, with its comprehensive menu of traditional Tuscan fare, or Ristorante Santa Elisabetta, with its extensive regional offerings.

FINE POINTS

Rooms: 96 rooms, 14 of them suites (7 junior suites and 7 regular suites).

Food: Free daily breakfast; lunch and dinner at Osteria della Pagliazza; Ristorante Santa Elisabetta is open for breakfast exclusively for guests staying in the suites, and it offers tasty dinners and wine tastings for all clients and the general public; wine tastings with sommelier; beer, wine, cocktails, and finger food also available at Florence Tower Bar; 24-hour room service.

Special Features: Fitness studio with Techno gym equipment; free Wi-Fi for all guests; fully handicapped and wheelchair accessible; meeting rooms and halls for weddings and other special events; bike rental; valet car parking; same-day laundry, ironing, and dry cleaning; smoking areas; small pets allowed in rooms; dog kits; services for infants and children include babysitting, kettles, cots, high chairs, and bottle warmers; full-service concierge; personal shopper; transfer fees from all Italian airports and elsewhere vary.

HOTEL BYRON

Viale E. Morin, 46, 55042 | Forte dei Marmi LU, Italy

Tel: +39 0584787052 | Fax: +39 0584787152

E-mail: info@hotelbyron.net

Website: www.hotelbyron.net

HOTEL BYRON is located in Forte dei Marmi on one of the pristine white-sand beaches that dot the Versilia coast along the Tyrrhenian Sea. One of the most famous vacation destinations in the world, the region has long attracted nobility, diplomats, businessmen, artists, and celebrities, who have built splendid homes amid the lush pinewoods and along the scenic beaches. Hotel Byron was originally one of these villas, commissioned during the first half of the 20th century by the charismatic and cosmopolitan José "Pepito" Caferino Canevaro, Duke of Zoagli, as a spot for family and friends to spend their holidays. Today, this charming seaside retreat continues to welcome visitors from around the world who seek refined accommodations amid relaxed surroundings. Individually decorated with soothing colors, quality linens, and elegant furnishings, the rooms overlook either the sea or the hotel's private garden with a view of the Apuan Alps in the distance. Hardwood floors, marble accented bathrooms, direct-line photos, satellite TV, and minibar are just a few of the additional amenities. Apart from the beauty of its beaches, gardens, and old town, Forte dei Marmi is also known for its elegance and sophistication: its shops and haute couture boutiques are as much of a magnet for tourists as the nearby historic cities of Florence, Pisa, and Arezzo, and its bars and restaurants attract bon vivants from around the globe. Of course, you don't have to leave the property for a bit of dolce vita: The on-site bar serves beer, wine, and cocktails to match its convivial atmosphere, and in the Michelin-starred La Magnolia restaurant, Chef Cristoforo Trapani creates seasonally changing regional specialties with a personal touch, using only the freshest ingredients from local producers. Enjoy dinner inside, by the pool, or on the expansive terrace, accompanied by top-notch service and the finest wines.

FINE POINTS

Rooms: 13 classic rooms, 7 deluxe rooms, 5 junior suites, 1 Shelly suite, 2 Byron suites, 1 single room.

Food: Breakfast, lunch, and dinner at La Magnolia restaurant; bar and lounge, which moves poolside in the warmer months.

Special Features: Outdoor swimming pool; free Wi-Fi throughout hotel; bicycles available at the hotel; close proximity to tennis courts and horseback riding; cooking classes; 2.5 miles to Versilia 18-hole golf course; 24-hour front desk; multilingual staff; just minutes to the Forte dei Marmi train station and Versilia motorway exit; half hour to the Pisa G. Galilei airport.

HOTEL HOME FLORENCE

Piazza Piave, 3 | 50122 Firenze, Italy

Tel: +39 055243668

E-mail: info@hhflorence.it

Website: www.hhflorence.com

HOTEL HOME FLORENCE is one of those little secrets that travelers-in-the-know love to pass along, a former villa situated on the Arno River that offers all the comforts of a home away from home in the historical city center of Florence. From the front door, it's a two-minute walk to the nearest bus stop, a seven-minute walk to the 15th-century Basilica of Santa Croce, a thirteen-minute walk to the Uffizi museum and gallery, and a scenic fifteen-minute walk along the river to the Ponte Vecchio. While the hotel's exterior is a model of Renaissance stateliness, its interiors are modern and minimalist, with a white and gold color palette serving as the backdrop to the chic furnishings and accessories provided by the renowned Cyrus Company interior designers. The rooms reflect this aesthetic, while imparting an air of luxurious comfort. Equally notable is the exclusive rooftop terrace, with stunning city views that are especially magical at night. While breakfast is served on-site daily, guests will need to explore the surrounding neighborhoods for lunch and dinner. A must-stop is La Carceri, a longtime top recommendation by the hotel's management and staff. Only a quick four-minute walk up the street to the Piazza Madonna della Neve, and located in the hip Oltrarno quarter, La Carceri is known for its authentic Italian fare, Neapolitan pizzas, handcrafted beers, and fine wines. The interior is rustic but cozy, with plastered walls on which guests are encouraged to graffiti, and a buzzing atmosphere due in part to the communal tables. You're a stranger for about five seconds here, and a lunch or dinner is guaranteed to be one of the highlights of your trip.

FINE POINTS

Rooms: 39 rooms, one of which is a suite.

Food: Free continental breakfast served on a communal table in the stylish breakfast lounge; the hotel highly recommends Le Carceri for lunch and dinner.

Special Features: Free welcome drink upon arrival; rooftop terrace; mezzanine with billiard tables; fitness center with gym and workout room; free Wi-Fi throughout hotel; meeting room; multilingual staff; laundry and dry cleaning; concierge; babysitting.

HOTEL PALAZZO BOCCI

Via Cavour, 17 | 06038 Spello (PG), Italy
Tel: +39 0742301021 | Fax: +39 0742301464
E-mail: info@palazzobocci.com
Website: www.palazzobocci.com

HOTEL PALAZZO BOCCI is positioned in the center of the charming town of Spello, one of the "pearls" of Italy's Middle Ages and also one of the Umbrian towns least crowded with tourists. Built in the 17th century and established as a hotel after meticulous restoration in 1992, Hotel Palazzo Bocci seamlessly blends history, tradition, and fine artwork with the latest in high-tech hospitality. Its fountain entrance, hanging gardens, spectacular Hall of Frescoes, and elegant rooms adorned with wooden beams, classic textiles, and frescoes all combine to create an atmosphere of refined beauty. Located near the center of town, it is also the perfect base from which to explore Spello and the nearby towns of Assisi and Perugia. Established as a Roman colony in the 1st century B.C., Spello bloomed in the early Middle Ages and is a marvel of that era's art and architecture. Of special note is its wealth of churches, many of them bearing artistic treasures such as the frescoes of Pinturicchio in the Baglioni Chapel in Santa Maria Maggiore. Rich in folkloric traditions as well, it is renowned for its Infiorata, the night of work spent creating the magnificent carpet of flowers for the Corpus Domini feast, and olive oil and bruschetta fair held each year in May. Spello is also dotted with many lovely shops and galleries selling traditional Umbrian arts and crafts and foodstuffs. Once back at the hotel, you can unwind from your explorations and share your discoveries with a drink in the bar or out on the lovely rooftop terrace. Located across the street, the hotel's restaurant, Il Molino, is considered one of the region's best-kept secrets. Exuding rustic elegance and warmth, it is neither touristy nor pretentious; instead the talented owner/chef Vania Buono and her sister, manager Francesca Buono, focus on producing nothing less than the fine art and craft of Umbrian cooking. Every item on the menu is delicious, and be sure to end your meal with something sweet—we recommend the Tiramisu al limone sfusato di Amalfi (Amalfi lemon Tiramisu) and a fine glass of Vin Santo.

FINE POINTS

Rooms: 23 rooms and 6 suites.

Food: Breakfast; two nearby enotecas (wine stores) on the same street that sell Italian wines including the local Montefalco as well as a selection of wonderful local cheeses and prosciuttos; Il Molino restaurant across the street (see restaurant reviews).

Special Features: All rooms are soundproofed and air-conditioned and feature hairdryer, telephone with direct line, color satellite TV, mini-bar and safe; high-speed Internet; reading lounge; bar/lounge; rooftop terrace; hanging garden; pets allowed.

HOTEL SAN MICHELE

Via Guelfa, 15 52044 | Cortona (Arezzo), Italy
Tel: +39 0575604348 | Fax: +39 0575630147
E-mail: info@hotelsanmichele.net
Website: www.hotelsanmichele.net

HOTEL SAN MICHELE is perfect for visitors seeking to immerse themselves in the history and ambiance of one of Italy's most storied cities. Established as an ancient Umbrian hillside settlement, Cortona was expanded by the Etruscans, occupied by the Romans, sacked by the Byzantines, sold to the Medicis, and awarded to the House of Lorraine before finally being welcomed into the Kingdom of Italy in the mid-nineteenth century. The building occupied by Hotel San Michele is one of the city's oldest, built in the center of town in the fifteenth century as a palace for the Baldelli family. Now a national monument as well as a hotel, it retains many of its original architectural details, including a beautifully preserved fresco of the Masaccio School. Accommodations include thirty-six rooms and five suites, each one individually decorated with antique furnishings and accessories. Hotel San Michele's centralized location means it is only minutes away from a host of must-see attractions, including the Diocesan Museum, with its second century Roman sarcophagus depicting the Battle of Dionysus and a fine collection of artworks by Renaissance masters such as Fra Angelico, Pietro Lorenzetti, Bartolomeo della Gatta, Luca Signorelli, and Sassetta. Take time to amble through the city streets and also explore the countryside, which offers plenty of adventures for avid hikers, horseback riders, and bicyclists. A newly built cycle track will guide you on a fascinating tour through past and present, starting with a visit to nearby Etruscan tombs and ending with a trek through a series of scenic neighboring villages. Gear up for whatever the day brings at the hotel's bountiful breakfast buffet, then wind down with a drink in the bar before heading back out to enjoy dinner at any one of a number of nearby restaurants.

FINE POINTS

Rooms: 36 rooms and 5 suites.

Food: Extensive daily breakfast buffet from 7:30 a.m. to 10:00 a.m; bar and lounge; room service.

Special Features: Massages, cooking classes, and bicycle tours by appointment; nearby sporting centers, spas, and wellness centers; 5 golf courses within a 30-minute drive; mountain biking, horseback riding, and hiking within the vicinity; an hour's drive or less from Firenze, Siena, Perugia, Pienza, Montepulciano, Montalcino, Arezzo, Assisi, Gubbio, Orvieto, and Spoleto; 24-hour front desk; laundry and ironing services; free Wi-Fi throughout hotel; business center; Sant'Agostino Conference Centre located next door; babysitting available; multilingual staff; private parking facilities.

HOTEL VILLA FIESOLE

Via Beato Angelico, 35 | 50014, Fiesole (FI)
Tel: +39 055597252 | Fax: +39 055599133
E-mail: info@villafiesole.it
Website: www.villafiesole.com

HOTEL VILLA FIESOLE, located in the heart of an ancient hilltop village, offers four-star accommodations for travelers seeking the peace and quiet of the Tuscan countryside but with quick and easy access to Florence. Founded as an Etruscan settlement sometime between the eighth and ninth centuries BC, Fiesole is today incorporated into the greater metropolitan area of Florence, approximately five miles from that city's center. The village retains all the charm of its ancient heritage, from the Roman amphitheater that is still in use today, to its narrow streets with quintessential medieval architecture and immaculately kept gardens. The hotel itself is located within a refurbished nineteenth-century villa, with lush grounds, scenic swimming pool, and views of Florence and the Arno. Each of the thirty-two guest rooms have been meticulously designed and furnished to ensure a comfortable and relaxing stay. No two are exactly alike: some have lovely frescoed ceilings; others offer magnificent views of Florence; and others have a private terrace or a small patio on the inner courtyard. All rooms are air conditioned, and include bathrooms with tubs and showers, slippers and bathrobes, and hairdryers. Mini bars, safes, and LCD televisions with preselected satellite and SKY TV channels round out the amenities. The views for which the property is famous are also enjoyable from the expansive terrace that fronts the La Terrazza restaurant. From April through October, dining al fresco on this sunny, flower-filled spot with views for miles is sure to be the highlight of your day. Start off with the complimentary breakfast buffet, and then drop by at lunch and dinner for perfectly prepared Tuscan and Mediterranean specialties. For an extra special treat, wait until the sun goes down and enjoy a romantic candlelit dinner against the backdrop of the lights of Florence sparkling in the distance.

FINE POINTS

Rooms: 32 rooms.

Food: Complimentary daily breakfast 7:30 a.m. to 10:30 a.m.; bar and lounge; lunch and dinner at La Terrazza restaurant; room service.

Special Features: Non-smoking rooms on request; scenic outdoor pool and hot tub; tennis courts; free Wi-Fi throughout property; dry cleaning and laundry service; self-serve laundry; banquet and meeting rooms; business center; newspaper service; concierge; multilingual staff; babysitting; pet friendly; free parking.

LE SILVE DI ARMENZANO,
ROMANTIK HOTEL & FARM HOUSES

Armenzano, 89 - 06081 - Assisi - PG | Italy
Tel: +39 0758019000 | Fax: +39 0758019005
E-mail: info@lesilve.it
Website: www.lesilve.it

Le Silve di Armenzano, Romantik Hotel & Farm Houses is the perfect spot for nature lovers seeking to immerse themselves in the idyllic beauty of the Umbrian countryside while enjoying top-notch accommodations and service. Getting there is no casual undertaking, but upon arrival it's clear that the incredibly steep and winding road up Mt. Subasio is worth the drive. A former tenth-century estate, it was discovered at the verge of ruin in 1977 by Giuseppe Sirignani, who renovated it into an exceptional hotel and farmstead. Today, Giuseppe's son Marco Sirignani continues his father's vision. Situated in the verdant hills of Umbria at the foot of Parco del Subasio near Assisi, the hotel is surrounded by forests and pastures that are home to an abundance of wildlife as well as a working farm—and its expansiveness allows for endless hikes and walks. A pool and tennis courts are also located on-site. Our time at Le Silve allowed for a peaceful and scenic spot to recharge and enjoy Umbria's myriad charms. The beautiful stone buildings hold rooms that impart the rich history of the region, while the hilltop site provides views onto an incredible panorama of endlessly unfolding countryside. The historic town of Assisi is just a short drive away as well. In terms of culinary experiences, every meal was excellent. Le Silve's young chef practices the tenets of Zero km cooking, which means all of the dishes feature ingredients grown or raised on the farm, or sourced locally. He clearly has real talent for showcasing Umbrian culinary delicacies with an exquisite convergence between the flavors of this great tradition and the quality farm production of the Le Silve country estate. And his handmade pastas were delectable works of art, especially the caramella.

FINE POINTS

Rooms: 19 rooms and 3 farmhouses.

Food: Breakfast, lunch, and dinner at Armentum restaurant.

Special Features: Swimming pool, garden, park, and tennis courts; wellness center with sauna; free Wi-Fi throughout hotel; immersive activities include birding and wildlife tours, culinary and photography courses, Nordic walking and guided walking tours, mountain biking and quad riding, and assisting with the day-to-day operations of the farm; mini-golfing, and farm life classes for the kids; 24 hour reception; laundry; babysitting upon request; variety of farm-produced products for sale.

LOCANDA IN TUSCANY

Moro Fiacchi, 13 53023 | Castiglione D'Orcia (SI), Italy

Tel: +39 05771700221

E-mail: info@locandaintuscany.com

Website: www.locandaintuscany.com

LOCANDA IN TUSCANY is a labor of love for owners Luca and Claudia Bernetti, who upon deciding to open a hotel asked themselves: "What is the luxury world missing today?" They knew a magnificent property with breathtaking views would not be enough. The Bernettis wanted their guests to fall in *love*. Locanda was the place where that could happen, where they could offer visitors a gift to carry in their hearts forever. Located in the scenic Val d'Orcia, a UNESCO World Heritage Center and the embodiment of Tuscan culture, the Locanda is not just a place to stay. Instead, the Bernettis and their staff have created an intimate and immersive experience of the beauty and vitality of life in the region, with a focus on sustainable and organic principles, from the paints used throughout the property to the mini-bar selections to the food and wine offerings. There are only nine rooms, each one an oasis crafted from traditional elements like brick floors, wood-beam ceilings, exposed stone walls, harmonious colors, and antique furnishings. To ensure a restful night's sleep, the all-wooden beds handcrafted by local artisans are outfitted with your choice of linen, satin, or cotton sheets. Rest and relaxation is also on the menu for daytime, when you can lounge by the panoramic pool or recharge with an Ayurvedic-based therapy, beauty treatment, or massage, all of which are available at the onsite wellness suite, Kama, or in the privacy of your room. The Bernettis are well acquainted with everything the area has to offer, and delight in helping their guests plan a hiking, biking, or running excursion in the surrounding countryside or introducing them to the culinary treasures hidden away in the surrounding vineyards and farms. Their hospitality extends to the very end of the day with a meal at the Taverna di Mozart, which showcases traditional Tuscan fare accompanied by the best local wines in an intimate atmosphere. After an evening sharing good food, good wine, and good conversation with your fellow travelers, the love affair will be complete.

FINE POINTS

Rooms: 9 rooms

Food: Breakfast, lunch, and dinner at Taverna di Mozart restaurant; room service.

Special Features: Kama wellness suite with series of Ayurvedic-based relaxation and beauty treatments; evening WATSU (water shiatsu) treatments and yoga classes by the panoramic outdoor pool; sun beds and umbrellas; wedding and event planning can accommodate 60 people in the Taverna di Mozart restaurant and up to 200 people in the garden; wine and food tours; cooking classes from one to three days with Michelin-starred chef; easy access to hiking, biking, and running trails; free Wi-Fi throughout property; concierge; multilingual staff; pet friendly; babysitting; free parking and airport transportation.

MAREPINETA RESORT

Viale Dante, 40, 48015 | Milano Marittima RA, Italy

Tel: +39 0544992263

E-mail: booking@marepinetaresort.com

Website: www.marepinetaresort.com

MAREPINETA RESORT, built in the 1920s and set in the heart of a lush green forest on the Adriatic coast, has been transformed into a contemporary architectural masterpiece by the prestigious architectural firm Studio Lissoni of Milan. Its goal was to retain the spirit of the original resort and setting while reinterpreting the luxury hotel concept. The resort is comprised of two structures, the first being the historic main building known as Casa Madre, or the "Mother House." This houses the lobby, conference center, reading room, lounge and bar, restaurant, and eighty-six rooms that have retained their 1927 charm, but updated with fine ceramics, luxury finishes, and breathtaking views of the woods or the sea. Twelve deluxe rooms and four junior suites were added in 2012 by the Lissoni firm and are thoroughly modern in their style and furnishings, enhanced by light woods and large windows. Directly connected to Casa Madre is the Villa Regina, whose aesthetic harmoniously blends contemporary elegance, privacy, and access to the great outdoors. The stunning scenery of MarePineta Resort, with its exclusive private beach, its large pool, its gardens, and its woods, offers infinite possibilities to create special moments, whether an intimate dinner for two or a celebratory event with friends and family. An open gym features state-of-the art Technogym equipment, as well as a mini club for children. There are two restaurants— one at the hotel and one on the beach—whose menus reflect star chef Andrea Ribaldone's tenet of "100 percent fresh, Italian, and simple." Whether he is reinterpreting a traditional dish or inventing what is sure to become an international classic, Ribaldone utilizes only the finest local ingredients. The skilled sommelier has carefully created a wine menu to complement Ribaldone's creations, while the front-of-the-house team excels at attentive but unobtrusive service that is as seamless as the elegant atmosphere.

FINE POINTS

Rooms: 165 rooms, including 5 junior suites and 2 regal suites.

Food: Complimentary American-style buffet breakfast; lunch at beachside restaurant; lunch and dinner at main restaurant.

Special Features: All rooms offer top-notch amenities, with free Wi-Fi, air conditioning, heating, satellite TV, minibar, telephone, safe, and spacious baths with shower or bath, a hair dryer, and vanity kit; exclusive Beach Club MarePineta, with umbrellas and chaise lounges; outdoor swimming pool; children's pool and mini club; tennis courts; beach gym; bike excursions; short walk to the seaside 27-hole Adriatic Golf Club, with green fees paid at hotel.

PALAZZO GUISCARDO

Via Provinciale di Vallecchia 16 | 55045 Pietrasanta (Lu)
Tel: +39 0584792914 | Fax: +39 0584735298
E-mail: info@palazzoguiscardo.it
Website: www.palazzoguiscardo.it

PALAZZO GUISCARDO is located in the charming Tuscan town of Pietrasanta along a stretch of Tuscan beach and resort towns known as the Versilia. Situated in an original Liberty-style building that dates back to the 1800s, this intimate hotel with the welcoming atmosphere of a private home has the added advantage of being just a few kilometers from the Mediterranean. The individually decorated bedrooms and suites are all furnished with beautiful fabrics and various period pieces; each item has been chosen to create a pleasingly warm environment. State-of-the-art features like 26-inch televisions, Internet access, Jacuzzis, sauna-showers, and Turkish baths enhance the traditional appeal. Particular care has been given to the bathrooms, all of which are spacious and outfitted with precious local marbles that give each of the rooms its name. Because of its seaside location, the hotel offers guests privileged access to the private Bagno Sandra beach. With only 32 tents and 20 sun umbrellas, your days spent lounging on the white sands, dipping in the azure sea, and soaking in the aromas of the nearby wild flowers and tamarind trees are guaranteed to be truly relaxing and rejuvenating. When you have had your fill of the beach and feel like some exercise, you can work out in the hotel's gym. If relaxation is on your mind, book a massage or enjoy a good book in many of the lovely spots in the garden, which also has a ping-pong table. Another of the hotel's distinguishing features is its bountiful breakfast, which can be served in-room or enjoyed in the charming breakfast room, and includes a selection of jams, honeys from nearby Borgo dei Medici farms, breads, croissants, cakes and patisserie, Tuscan cold cuts, fruit, cheeses, and yoghurt.

FINE POINTS

Rooms: 9 rooms, of which 1 is a suite and 4 are junior suites.

Food: A bountiful breakfast served either in-room or in the lovely breakfast room. Nearby restaurants.

Special Features: 24/7 concierge service; air conditioning; satellite television; safe; mini bar; complimentary Internet access in the rooms and Wi-Fi in the lobby; elevator; laundry; parking; privileged access to the best restaurants and beaches; gym; ping-pong; transfers to and from Pisa and Florence airports upon request; guided art tours; motorboat excursions; concierge can also arrange cooking and sculpture classes, language lessons, and massages, as well as plan tailor-made holiday packages for guests.

PALAZZO MANFREDI

RELAIS &
CHATEAUX.

Via Labicana, 125 | 00184 Rome, Italy
Tel: +39 0677591380 | Fax: +39 067005638
E-mail: info@hotelpalazzomanfredi.it
Website: www.palazzomanfredi.com/en/

PALAZZO MANFREDI is an oasis of modern-day chic that literally sits in the shadow of ancient Rome, just steps away from the magnificent Colosseum and its Ludus Magnus gladiator training school. Today this hip neighborhood, known as Monti, resonates with energy of a different kind, home to up-and-coming galleries, boutiques, and restaurants. And Palazzo Manfredi is the best spot from which to experience it. Occupying an elegant 17th-century villa, the hotel was the vision of Count Goffredo Manfredi, one of Italy's most famous entrepreneurs and construction magnates. In 2002 Manfredi refurbished the palazzo into a five-star luxury hotel that extends his family's tradition of warm hospitality to every guest who crosses the threshold of its front door. Some of the most notable names in contemporary design—including Igno Maurer, Van Egmond, Giorgia Dennerlein, Martin Margiela, and Philippe Starck—were brought in to customize the hotel's fourteen rooms and suites. Rich colors, exquisite textures, and the finest materials all impart an air of elegance and luxury. Few places in the city feature such intimate views of the Colosseum and the magnificent Oppian Hill gardens. Fewer still offer such exclusive amenities as those found in the hotel's most posh suite, whose luxurious bathroom is outfitted with a shower, steam room, chromotherapy sauna, whirlpool bath, and mini-gym. The hotel's restaurant, Aroma, is equally indulgent. Of course, its views of the Colosseum are unmatched—from sunup with morning coffee to sundown with an evening aperitif, they never fail to thrill—but you don't earn a 5 Star Diamond and Michelin star without also having demonstrated some serious culinary chops. This is the kind of restaurant where people fall in love, get engaged, celebrate major life events, and enjoy some of the most exquisite cuisine currently being served in the city.

FINE POINTS

Rooms: 14 rooms, including 2 suites.

Food: Breakfast, lunch, and dinner at Aroma restaurant, bar, and lounge; room service.

Special Features: Special stay packages; complimentary bottle of prosecco and box of chocolates upon check-in; Free Wi-Fi throughout hotel; multilingual staff; concierge; ticket booking for Rome's major museums and events; guided tours of the major sites; dry cleaning and laundry service; meeting and banquet room; babysitting; airport transportation

PARK HOTEL AI CAPPUCCINI

Via Tifernate | 06024 Gubbio (PG), Italy

Tel: +39 0759234 | Fax: +39 0759220323

E-mail: info@parkhotelaicappuccini.it

Website: www.parkhotelaicappuccini.it

PARK HOTEL AI CAPPUCCINI is located in the heart of Umbria in the small community of Gubbio. An important historical site, Gubbio is home to the second largest set of ancient Roman theater ruins existing today. The town was also an epicenter of religious activity during the medieval era, sending over 1,000 knights to fight in the Crusades. The Park Hotel ai Cappuccini itself is located inside a 17th-century Capuchin monastery, and it pays tribute to this heritage with its beautifully preserved architecture and grounds. Inside, a fusion of modern and traditional furnishings, artworks, and ambiance create an air of cultured elegance, while the capable and caring staff ensure that every guest feels right at home. Over the years, the owners have accumulated an impressive series of artworks that include 15th-century frescos, Renaissance paintings, Flemish tapestries and furniture, as well as modern sculptures and posters. Great care has been given to their placement throughout the hotel, providing guests with a unique opportunity to enjoy pieces usually found only in museums and galleries. Ninety-two rooms, including junior and regular suites, are available in the monastery and in its modern addition. Plus, the recently renovated Villa Benveduti, located nearby, is an enchanting setting for memorable events as well as intimate groups to stay in its ten well-appointed rooms. The Cappuccini Wellness Center offers restorative therapies based on the ancient monastic tradition of medicinal plant cultivation, mixed with the latest in modern technologies. The newly opened indoor water park is an architectural delight, designed by Simone Micheli as a water-based fantasy land with its matrix of playful shapes and bright colors. It is also a serious place in which to enjoy a number of hydrotherapies, including hydro massage and thalasso. Exceptional Italian and international cuisine is offered at the Nicolao restaurant, where guests dine in Old World ambiance under rafted ceilings and walls decorated with historic artworks. The original monastery's water catchment room has been transformed into the La Cisterna wine cellar, housing the hotel's extensive variety of wines, champagnes, and locally produced honeys, jams, truffle sauces, cereals, oil, cheese, and cold cuts.

FINE POINTS

Rooms: 92 rooms, including junior and regular suites. 10 rooms in Villa Beneveduti.

Food: A la carte breakfast, lunch, and dinner at Nicolao. Wines and local foodstuffs available for purchase and tastings at La Cisterna wine cellar. Bar offering beer, wine, and cocktails. Room service available.

Special Features: Full-service wellness center featuring variety of natural plant therapies, Finnish sauna, Turkish bath, and Raxul thermal bath room; water park with lap pools, children's pool, and variety of mineral water hydro massage and thalasso therapies; fitness center with isotonic Technogym machines, Pilates classes, and tennis courts; pharmacy selling local teas, spirits, and other remedies utilizing local recipes and ingredients; nearby trails for horseback riding, hiking, and mountain biking; free parking; shuttle bus service into Gubbio.

PARK HOTEL VILLA GRAZIOLI

Via Umberto Pavoni, 19 | 00046 Grottaferrata (Rome), Italy
Tel: +39 069454001 | Fax: +39 069413506
E-mail: info@villagrazioli.com
Website: www.villagrazioli.com

PARK HOTEL VILLA GRAZIOLI sits majestically on the outskirts of Rome at the foot of Tusculum Hill just outside Frascati. Its locale showcases expansive views of the surrounding urban areas, as well the Tyrrhenian Sea, whose surface glistens like a polished sheet of glass in the distance. Once a meeting place for artists, poets, architects, and other famous personalities, including the Marquis de Sade (who describes the house in his writings as one of the most elegant in the region), this sixteenth-century masterpiece was eventually abandoned. Rescued from complete neglect in 1987 by the Company Villa Grazioli, the property underwent a thorough restoration of its architecture, decor, and 15,000 square foot park and gardens. Today, this Italian National Monument is also a sixty-two-room hotel that provides architecture and history buffs with a fascinating ambiance while at the same time serving as a comfortable and stylish retreat from the urban hustle and bustle. The hotel is noted for its beautifully preserved frescoes, created over three periods, which decorate the floors and ceilings of the main floor, including an entire gallery named after that room's painter, Giovanni Paolo Pannini. It is also famous for the view from its rooftop terrace, which is reached by a spiral staircase in the west wing. While located 21 km from Rome, a train ride from the hotel and back effortlessly puts you in the thick of the city. The surrounding towns of Frascati and Grottaferatta are also well worth a visit as they feature fine shops and restaurants with authentic local Roman (Lazio-Regional) cuisine. Within the hotel itself, the Acquaviva restaurant complements the refined historic ambiance with exquisitely prepared Mediterranean food and the region's most famous and traditional wines.

FINE POINTS

Rooms: 62 rooms in total, 13 of which are in the main villa and the rest are located in two restored eighteenth-century cottages, Paggeria and Limonaia, which are connected to the main villa through two underground corridors.

Food: Bar; breakfast and lunch; dinner at Acquaviva restaurant.

Special Features: Air-conditioned rooms with satellite TV; Wi-Fi throughout entire hotel, purchased by the hour or day; banquet facilities for weddings cocktail parties, and special events of up to 200 people; parking for up to 120 cars; swimming pool; lush park and gardens; free hourly shuttles to and from the hotel to Frascati train station; special arrangement with the Castel Gandolfo Golf Club (10 km from hotel) and with a wellness center (2 km from hotel) featuring fitness, steam bath, sauna, Jacuzzi, indoor pool, massage, and beauty center.

RELAIS & CHATEAUX IL FALCONIERE

Loc. San Martino | 370 52044 | Cortona AR | Italy
Tel: +39 0575612679 | Fax: +39 0575612927
E-mail: info@ilfalconiere.it
Websites: www.ilfalconiere.com | www.baracchiwinery.com

RELAIS & CHATEAUX IL FALCONIERE is an exclusive and beautifully restored seventeenth-century villa nestled among vineyards in the heart of the Tuscan countryside in Cortona. Once home to famous nineteenth-century poet Antonio Guadagnoli, today Il Falconiere is under the capable ownership of Silvia and Riccardo Baracchi, who inherited the property from his grandmother. The couple and their adult son, Benedetto, continue the family tradition that began in 1860 of cultivating the vines that produce their outstanding wines, while creating an extraordinary luxury experience for travelers. Just as you would never expect guests in your home to fend for themselves, neither do the Baracchis. They graciously receive every guest and ensure all their needs are met. Silvia welcomed us as if we were old friends, and wouldn't think of letting us remain hungry after our long journey. Although the restaurant was closed, she soon seated us for a light alfresco meal, served on the finest china and crystal. The highly capable staff are equally warm and attentive, and every corner of the property is designed to conjure the same spirit, especially the intimate, elegantly furnished guest rooms with their original antiques, wrought iron or four poster beds, and fine fabrics. The property is also notable for its wonderful Thesan Etruscan spa and indoor and outdoor swimming pools. It is also a great base from which to explore the countryside by bicycle. After one exhilarating 60km ride, we returned home knowing we had truly earned that evening's meal. Silvia is an amazingly talented chef whose outstanding cuisine has earned their restaurant a Michelin star. We recommend sitting out on the terrace, with its candlelit tables, fine tableware, impeccable service, and quintessential "Under the Tuscan Sun" views. Not only were we served outstanding regional cuisine, we were privileged to taste some truly remarkable wines, including their 2007 Ardito and 2008 Sangiovese, both of which won the Decanter Worldwide Award in 2011.

Rooms: 22, including 10 classic rooms, 3 deluxe, 6 junior suites, and 3 suites—located in the Villa or by the Chapel overlooking the vineyards. There are two suites, one classic and one junior, located near the Thesan Etruscan Spa.

Food: Award winning Michelin Restaurant located in the old lemon tree house with two levels and three rooms: the main dining area, another more private and intimate with only five tables, and the exclusive little clocks room with just one table. Dine by candlelight in the open-air on the panoramic terrace, weather permitting. For special events customized menus with wine pairing available.

Winery: Baracchi Winery with its vineyards and wine cellar are set within the estate.

Special Features: Air-conditioned rooms; Thesan Etruscan Spa with indoor and outdoor swimming pools, Jacuzzi, sauna, solarium, aromatherapies, and massages, including specialty olive oil and wine massage, stone therapy, Fango, boue, and revitalizing, anti-stress, anti-aging, and anti-rheumatism treatments; mountain biking; horseback riding; wine and estate tours tours; cooking classes that include complimentary apron and recipe book; nine-hole golf nearby; valet parking and car park; dogs accepted; lift and elevator; dedicated Internet access; Wi-Fi hot spot; car transfer service.

FINE POINTS

RELAIS LA CORTE DEI PAPI

Via La Dogana, 12 | 52044 Cortona (Arezzo) | Loc. Pergo
Tel: +39 0575614109 | Fax: +39 0575614963 | Cell: +39 3453406860
E-mail: info@lacortedeipapi.com
Website: www.lacortedeipapi.com

RELAIS LA CORTE DEI PAPI rests in the heart of Tuscany's rolling hills that border Umbria, within a few minutes from Cortona. This small town of ancient origins has preserved its appeal as an antique medieval village. It's the ideal spot to enjoy a family vacation within a peaceful setting surrounded by nature and near small villages, "cities of art," and breathtaking landscapes. Once a seventeenth-century historic dwelling and residence of the current owners, the Papi family, it has been skillfully restored using the existing antique materials or utilizing similar ones obtained locally. Today, Relais La Corte dei Papi is a magnificent infusion of superior elegance and charm, reflecting David Papi's passion for providing top fine dining and hospitality experiences. The garden, with a swimming pool and gazebo, are gracefully encompassed by the relais, creating an exclusive setting of pure relaxation. The hotel offers five different types of accommodations, from guestrooms to a spacious and exclusive suite with a private in-room spa. All are decorated with warm antique furnishings and modern comforts. David Papi appears to be in all places, all the time. He's a Houdini in his own right, showing up at receptions to offer assistance with a day of tours and excursions, poolside to be sure you have sufficient towels or drinks, or even during dinner to pair the perfect wine with your selections. Restaurant La Corte dei Papi's chefs will dazzle you as they prepare Tuscan cuisine with a contemporary touch — fresh pasta, bread, and desserts are all made from scratch. The silverware, the prized porcelain, and delicate Flanders linen unite with first class service to envelope you in a romantic and luxurious setting.

FINE POINTS

Rooms: 15 rooms, to include deluxe double room, deluxe cottage, classic junior suite, deluxe suite spa, and exclusive suite spa.

Food: Bar; La Corte dei Papi restaurant, featuring creative and traditional Tuscan cuisine, Fusion, vegetarian, and seafood; all open to public.

Special Features: Swimming pool; garden; parking; cooking lessons; wine tour; organization of guided tours and excursions; laundry and ironing service; limousine service; car rental.

RELAIS TODINI RESIDENZA D'EPOCA

Frazione Collevalenza - 06050 | Todi (PG), Italy
Tel: +39 075887521 | Fax: +39 075887182
E-mail: relais@relaistodini.com
Website: www.relaistodini.com
Skype: relais.todini.todi

RELAIS TODINI RESIDENZA D'EPOCA is a hotel of distinction, steeped in the history and beauty of its surroundings while also accommodating the discerning traveler's every need. Perched atop a hillside in Umbria amid 3,200 scenic acres, the property is distinguished by a former 14th-century manor house, whose architectural roots go back to Etruscan/Roman times, and 740 acres of vineyards, all of which is under family ownership. Indeed, an atmosphere of welcoming warmth permeates the property, whose interiors are decorated with period pieces augmented by rich tapestries, cozy fireplaces, stone and terracotta floors, and frescoed walls. The twelve rooms, which include four suites, are likewise luxuriously outfitted. Guests who call and request a room with a view are happily told, "Of course, our pleasure!" Upon arrival, guests are delighted to realize their request was superfluous—the Relais Todini's hilltop position offers 360-degree views from every imaginable spot, indoors and out. The sparkling outdoor pool is the perfect spot from which to relax either before or after a treatment at the on-site Spa Skin and Co Relais Todini, a wellness center that also includes a Turkish bath, outdoor Jacuzzi, and a bathtub for wine therapy managed by an expert staff proficient in a wide range of personalized treatments, from hot-stone massage to truffle therapy. Take your massage to the next level by enjoying it *al fresco* in an open-sided cabana that allows you to enjoy spectacular views as your cares melt away. And you don't have to miss a workout, either, thanks to the on-site fitness center, which also includes a Turkish bath and outdoor Jacuzzi. Extend the day's pleasures into the evening with dinner at the on-site restaurant. Known for its elegant interiors and spectacular patio dining, this world-class venue blends international cuisine with regional Umbrian specialties and a wine list that includes vintages from the on-site Cantina Todini winery.

FINE POINTS

Rooms: 12 rooms—3 superior suites, 1 regular suite, 6 superior rooms, and 2 classic rooms.

Food: Breakfast, lunch, and dinner at the on-site restaurant.

Special Features: Wi-Fi throughout property; outdoor swimming pool; wellness and beauty center with Jacuzzi, Turkish Bath, massage, and variety of treatments; fitness center; tennis court; park and garden; hiking and mountain biking through vineyards, olive groves, and forests; banquet and meeting rooms; heliport and shuttle bus service; tours and tastings of on-site Cantina Todini winery; cooking classes in the private Villa Sant'Isidoro; front desk can arrange visits to nearby cities of Todi, Orvieto, Gubbio, Assisi, and Perugia.

RELAIS TORRE MOZZA

Torre Mozza, 3 | 57025 Piombino (LI), Italy

Tel: +39 0565252102

E-mail: info@relaistorremozza.com

Website: www.relaistorremozza.com/en/

RELAIS TORRE MOZZA, located in a former fortified watch-tower, is the next best thing to renting a private seaside retreat. Built in the 16th century by the famed Appiani family of Piombino to monitor the transport and unloading of minerals from the nearby island of Elba, the property now serves as a boutique hotel for travelers seeking an intimate white sand beach experience along with luxury service and amenities. Featuring eight elegantly decorated suites, each with a sea view and one with terrace and Jacuzzi inside the room, the hotel is designed to encourage daily communion with the forces of sand and sea. With your feet in the water and your gaze on the horizon, you will instantly feel yourself relax and unwind in tune with the gentle breezes, the ebb and flow of the surf, the scent of the water, and the views that stretch across the Tyrrhenian Sea to Elba shimmering in the distance. Unwind with a day spent at the beach or on the rooftop terrace, with its sundeck, Jacuzzi, and expansive views of the entire archipelago. Limited to only two people at a time, this intimate space is the perfect spot to receive a relaxing massage or to enjoy a pre- or post-dinner aperitif. Situated among some of the most distinctive of the Maremma's natural environments, the hotel also makes a great base from which to explore the coastal nature preserves of Sterpaia Park and Rimigliano, with their mix of sand dunes, grassland habitats, juniper thickets, and pine woods. Refuel after your adventures with a meal at the on-site restaurant, whose chef transforms the bounty of earth and sea into a gastronomic experience that is at once innovative and yet true to its Tuscan roots.

FINE POINTS

Rooms: 8 suites.

Food: Breakfast from 8:30 a.m to 10:30 a.m.; dinner at on-site restaurant; room service.

Special Features: All suites are air conditioned and feature flat screen televisions and fully outfitted bathrooms with shower, hairdryer, and toiletries; direct access to beach with beach beds and umbrellas; private terrace with Jacuzzi situated on top of the tower; sitting areas; massage services; water sports facilities; hiking in the area; meeting and event facilities and planning; laundry service; concierge; multilingual staff; free Wi-Fi throughout; free private parking.

RELAIS VILLA MONTE SOLARE

Via Montali 7 | 06068 Tavernelle di Panicale | Perugia, Italy
Tel: +39 075832376 | Fax: +39 0758355462
E-mail: info@villamontesolare.com
Website: www.ldcitalianhotels.com/en/hotels/villa-monte-solare/

RELAIS VILLA MONTE SOLARE is a peaceful retreat on a magnificent estate in the Umbrian countryside. Surrounded by breathtaking views of rolling hills lined with olive groves, vineyards, and Cyprus trees, this resort is the embodiment of Italy's green heart. Once home to Italian aristocracy, Villa di Monte Solare dates back to the 18th century and is bedecked with marble fireplaces, ornate furniture, lavish fabrics, and terracotta flooring. These features preserve a sense of the hotel's history while establishing an air of refinement and elegance. Guests can stay in the rooms and suites within the villa, or in one of the rustic farmhouses on the property, all of which afford excellent views of the landscape. Options for cultural exploration abound; the ultra-historic village of Assisi is an hour's drive, and Perugia, the modern-day cultural capital of Umbria, is even closer. At the resort, an extensive trail system is an excellent way for runners or walkers to explore the grounds, while the pool and tennis courts provide additional recreational options. For those intrigued by the region's culinary traditions, the cooking classes and truffle hunting excursions are a great way to broaden one's knowledge of Italian cuisine and cooking. Small classes allow participants to learn skills and prepare a delicious meal with master chefs and fellow foodies in the intimate La Capannina cooking school. Located in the limonaia, the historic lemon house within the resort's gardens, Le Muse Spa and Beauty Farm is Villa Monte Solare's private wellness sanctuary. With a wide array of high-end facilities and treatments, the spa specializes in personal attention, leaving guests feeling truly pampered. Showcasing the diverse bounty of Umbrian produce, Dolium restaurant's dishes centers around seasonal, regional ingredients, including truffles found in the area and the Relais's own olive oil. The restaurant serves all three meals and hosts a great selection of wines from the area and beyond. The excellent sommelier can help guests navigate the extensive list according to their tastes.

FINE POINTS

Rooms: 25 rooms.

Food: Lunch, dinner, and complimentary breakfast at Dolium restaurant; room service.

Special Features: Le Muse Spa and Beauty Farm with massage rooms, Turkish bath, hydrotherapy area, sauna, and facial and body treatments; outdoor pool; tennis courts; cooking classes and wine tastings; free Wi-Fi throughout property; business center and meeting rooms; babysitting; dry cleaning and laundry service; free parking; shuttle bus service.

TOSCANA RESORT CASTELFALFI

Loc. Castelfalfi | 50050 Montaione | Florence, Italy
Tel: +39 0571891000 | Fax: +39 0571891001
E-mail: info@castelfalfi.it
Website: www.castelfalfi.it

TOSCANA RESORT CASTELFALFI is an utterly immersive Tuscan experience, a luxury estate set on 2,700 acres of gorgeous hillside. Originally settled 2,500 years ago, Castelfalfi has been through several periods of prosper and ruin and was eventually abandoned altogether by its residents in the 1960s. The reincarnation of this historical property reflects an astonishing commitment to preserving the original architecture and landscape in accordance with modern sustainable building principals. Its agricultural heritage remains an essential component, and guests can tour the historic vineyards and olive groves, sample the cold-pressed olive oil from local producers, the wines of *Tenuta di Castelfalfi*, or go truffle hunting with a local expert. The village is home to a variety of shops, cafes, restaurants, accommodations, and recreational possibilities. Between its Mountain and Lake Courses, the renowned Golf Club Castelfalfi has a total of 27 holes, making it the largest course in Tuscany. Additional outdoor pursuits include horseback riding and an extensive hiking and biking trail network. The traditional Tuscan farmhouses have been carefully refurbished to include villas, townhouses, and apartments that are scattered across the estate. Among these residences also lies the charming Hotel La Tabaccaia, while Il Castelfalfi, a five-star hotel and spa constructed according to green principles, is set to open in March 2017. Castelfafi is home to three restaurants that highlight the prized culinary traditions of the area and showcase local ingredients. Helmed by Michelin-rated Chef Michele Rinaldi, La Rocca is located on the terrace of the medieval castle and serves excellent Tuscan fare with fabulous views of the surrounding area. Il Rosmarino is a more casual trattoria and bar, where Chef Francesco Ferreti prepares a large selection of Tuscan favorites and wood-fired pizzas. Chef Ferreti also oversees La Via del Sale, which offers authentic Italian cuisine distinguished by the freshest ingredients and handmade pastas. Enjoy incomparable Italian delicacies at the restaurant or just take in the panoramic views of the Tuscan landscape by dining al fresco. Opportunities to engage with the cuisine extend beyond the restaurants; the Rosso Toscano Cooking School offers an incredible array of classes taught by both chefs.

FINE POINTS

Opening: March 2017

Rooms: 150 rooms.

Food: Breakfast buffet at La Tabaccaia; refined cuisine at La Rocca and La Via del Sale; and casual dining at Il Rosmarino.

Special Features: Fitness center with gym, sauna, and massage; outdoor pool; tennis court; golf course; cooking classes and wine tastings; hunting; guided nature walks; horseback riding; quad rentals; children's activities; wedding services; free Wi-Fi throughout the resort; dry cleaning and laundry service; free parking.

VILLA LA MASSA

Via della Massa 24, 50012 Candeli | Florence, Italy

Tel: +39 05562611 | Fax: +39 055633102

E-mail: info@villalamassa.com

Website: www.villalamassa.com

VILLA LA MASSA is a sixteenth-century Medici palace surrounded by approximately twenty-two acres of landscaped gardens that is elegantly perched on the banks of the Arno River, only minutes from Florence and the famed Chianti wine region. It received new life as a hotel in 1950, with a careful restoration that retains its aristocratic Renaissance splendor. The staff is on top of every detail, yet their attention is discrete and never overwhelming. The grounds are beautiful, offering tranquil views of the Arno River countryside. A complimentary shuttle service takes you straight to the Ponte Vecchio, right into the heart of Florence city center—the best of all worlds! But don't let the elegance fool you—Villa La Massa is ideal for families, offering a host of indoor and outdoor activities. In addition, qualified babysitters are available with a twelve-hour notice. Staying put has rewards for the adults as well, with the Arno SPA. Aside from a wide range of massages,

there is an outdoor heated swimming pool in the garden with lounges for sunbathing, and a fitness centre that features the latest exercise machines. Nearby is a riding school; a tennis club with sixteen red clay courts; and jogging paths lined with fragrant olive trees along the Arno. The hotel provides mountain bikes, and the knowledgeable staff can advise on the most interesting routes into the countryside. Dining at the hotel's Il Verrocchio restaurant is under the direction of executive chef Andrea Quagliarella, who uses organic products from the villa's gardens. His inspiring menu is the perfect complement to the breathtaking views of the Arno and the Chianti hills. *Al fresco* dining on the terrace is a must during the warm months, giving you prime seats for stunning sunsets. Menus include both Tuscan and Mediterranean specialties accompanied by an impressive wine list representing 400 of the best Italian wines, with emphasis on Tuscan vintages.

FINE POINTS

Rooms: 37 rooms. The entire hotel may be rented for private use.

Food: Medicean Bar serving lunch; Il Verrocchio restaurant serving breakfast and dinner; wine cellar featuring wine and cheese pairings for private parties.

Special Features: Conference and banquet facilities for meetings, weddings, and other special events; private parking; internet access; Arno SPA with fitness and beauty center; babysitting service; outdoor swimming pool; variety of sporting activities nearby, including riding, tennis, jogging, and golf; kids' amenities; complimentary shuttle service to and from Florence (Ponte Vecchio).

Southern Italy

A land whose beauty encompasses everything from rugged mountains and craggy coastlines to white-sand beaches and stunning turquoise seas, Southern Italy attracts visitors who seek not only a luxury travel experience, but one that affords privacy as well. You can happily wander through dozens of historic towns and charming villages devoid of the usual throngs of tourists, or tuck yourself away in a chic Sardinian island resort. In fact, this island paradise, along with Sicily, perfectly balances hidden getaways with elite hot spots; it is only a matter of how much you wish to see or be seen. Whatever your choice, you can also count on the fact that your travels will be augmented by a local hospitality as warm and inviting as the ever present sun, all accompanied by plenty of the region's famously tempting food and drink.

Molise

This region is located in south-central Italy, between the Apennines and the Adriatic coast. Molise is known for its beautiful, natural wilderness and time-honored lifestyle. Its rolling hills are strewn with castles that overlook medieval villages and ancient ruins. It is divided into two provinces: Campobasso and Isernia. Campobasso, the capital, is well known for its procession of the "Mysteries," occurring during Holy Week and marked by a somber procession and passion plays. The streets of the town are full of activity, with masses of people who come from throughout Italy for the occasion. The Mysteries are living pictures enacted by men, women, and children, symbolically representing the major feasts of the Church and episodes from the Bible. The town of Isernia rises in the western part of Molise, and it dates back as far as the prehistoric era when the community of the first Europeans resided in one of its valleys. Isernia and its surrounding locales remain unscathed by tourism, preserving the anonymity and charm of an unrevealed Italy. Located in Isernia is the Museum of Santa Maria delle Monache, which includes two sections, one dedicated to the Paleolithic period and another to remains from the Samnite period. The town also contains the Sanctuary of St. Cosma and St. Damian, the Fraterna Fountain, St. Peter's Cathedral, and the adjacent entrance hall that comprises a part of the podium of a temple dating back to the Roman Republic. Each year in June, the donkey race takes place in the Venafro amphitheater, where contestants ride bareback donkeys and race in a circle. The craft shops of Isernia still create and sell their age-old flutes, bagpipes, and tambourines.

Not to be missed during your stay at the Grand Hotel Cocumella is a trip along the Amalfi Coast or a jaunt across the water to Capri on the hotel's very own authentic 1880 tall ship, the Vera.

Classic Cuisine: The Molisani were shepherds who journeyed with their herds to Puglia. Because they traveled often, their dishes reflect effortlessness in preparation and time. Consequently, vegetables and cheeses, along with pasta, grains, and fruits, are the key ingredients of their diets. The seasonings of Molise are primarily *il diavolillo* (hot chili peppers, garlic, olive oil, and tomatoes) as prepared in *spaghetti con aglio* and *olio e peperoncino*, which is a spaghetti with garlic, olive oil, and chili peppers. Unique to Molise are a white polenta, *P'lenta d'iragn,* prepared with potatoes and wheat and served with tomato sauce, and *Calconi di ricotta rustica, ravioli* stuffed with Ricotta and Provolone cheeses along with *prosciutto,* then fried in oil. The cheeses of Molise consist primarily of Manteca, Burrino, and Scamorza, or Scamorza *affumicate* (smoked version).

Classic Wines: Molise is a region that is covered in mountains. It produces very little wine, the vast majority of which is not DOC quality. There are four DOCs: Pentro de Isernia, Tintilia del Molise, Biferno, and Molise. Biferno is the best known, producing both reds and *rosatos.*

Classic Pairings: The *rosato*, a blend of Montelpulciano and Aglianico, is a great match for the region's traditional smoked and spiced dishes.

Campania

Renowned as the birthplace of pizza, spaghetti, and *Mozzarella di Bufalo* (Buffalo Mozzarella), Campania is also the region immediately below Lazio, and denotes the true beginning of southern Italy. It has always been a preferred destination, first by the Romans, who coined it the *campania felix* (fortunate countryside). Here, they established themselves in villas and palatial estates that stretched around the bay. The historical significance and renowned beauty of the Campania region is enthralling. Naples, the capital of this province, has numerous sites of cultural and artistic importance. It is home to an aquarium, zoo, Museum of Capodimonte, and the National Archaeological Museum, which houses the important finds of Pompeii and Herculaneum. Some of Italy's most renowned sites are located in this region: Mount Vesuvius, the ancient ruinous civilizations of Pompeii and Paestum, the stunning coast of Amalfi, and Sorrento's enchanting peninsula, full of fashionable boutiques, restaurants, and cafés. Days may be spent beach hopping, visiting the chic towns of Positano and Praiano, or taking road trips to the costal summits of Ravello to admire breathtaking views and the magnificent gardens of Villa Cimbrone and Villa Rufolo, the latter having been the inspiration for Wagner's *Parsifal*. Of course,

there are also the lovely islands of Capri, Ischia, and Procida, easily accessible for a one-day excursion or a weeklong sojourn.

Classic Cuisine: The volcanic soils of Campania grow some of the best produce in Italy, including San Marzano tomatoes, peppers, peaches, grapes, apricots, figs, oranges, and lemons. Its most famous cheeses are *Mozzarella di Bufalo*, as well as sheep's milk Pecorino, Scamorza, Mascarpone, and Ricotta. Although not native to the region, *Parmigiano Reggiano* is often incorporated into many of the most famous recipes. Moreover, Italian food would not be the same without Campania's spaghetti topped with *pommarola*, their famous tomato sauce; *pizza margherita* (Mozzarella, tomatoes, and basil); *calzone* (stuffed pizza); *caprese* (Mozzarella

and fresh sliced tomatoes with olive oil, basil, and ground pepper); and of course *parmigiana di melanzane* (eggplant Parmesan), just to highlight a few of their culinary contributions. The food reveals distinct influences by the various civilizations that have visited these shores throughout the centuries, particularly the French, Greek, Moorish, and Spanish. Along the coastline, seafood is prevalent with *fritto misto di mare*, a mixture of fish fried in olive oil, while other recipes use octopus, cuttlefish, squid, clams, or mussels and prepare them in their own distinct ways. One example is *spaghetti con le vongole in salsa bianca* (spaghetti with clams in white sauce) or *cozze in culla*, which are tomatoes that have been cut in half, the pulp scraped out and filled with capers, parsley, oregano, and bread crumbs. Save room at the end of your meal for *zuppa inglese alla napoletana*, made with Ricotta, chocolate, rum and Liqueur Galliano, Strega, or Amaretto.

Classic Wines: Campania has a long, rich history with the vine. In Ancient Rome, the Falernian from this area was one of the most well known and highest regarded wines in world, praised in ancient texts for its ability to age beautifully. Aglianico, which is a red grape usually used to produce mass amounts of bland wine, really shows well here. Taurasi DOCG and Aglianico del Taburno DOCG are excellent examples. Look for skilled producers Mastroberardino and Feudi di San Gregorio.

Classic Pairings: A slice of Neapolitan pizza is a bucket list achievement. To accompany the experience, the Fiano di Avellino DOCG produces full-bodied, intense whites from the Fiano grape.

Puglia

Also known as Apuglia, this region comprises the "heel" of the Italian boot, while the Gargano Peninsula is its "spur." Most travelers who venture this far south are taking a boat from Brindisi to Greece; however, this is a region full of enjoyable beaches and charming coastal towns. Its relatively flat terrain makes it an ideal region for biking. Bari is the capital and has preserved its ancient maritime traditions through the centuries. Polignano a Mare is a small and fascinating medieval town in the province of Bari on the Adriatic coast. Polignano presents spectacular caves formed as a result of the constant wave motion of the sea that shaped the calcareous rock. Some of the caves are so deep that they extend downward to the center of the town. The most interesting caves to visit are the Grotta Palazzese, Grotta Stalattitica, and the Grotta della Foca. Some signs of human existence have been found here that date back to the Paleolithic age. Alberobella is a magical land of elf-like, conical white-washed houses made of stones held together without mortar, called *trullis*. According to legend, there are two different versions explaining their construction. Some declare that the Counts of Puglia insisted the dwellings be made in this way, enabling them to be easily torn down should the tax inspectors come to collect money from occupants unable to pay. Others say because the residents only had to pay for permanent houses, the white stones on top of the roof could be easily removed, demonstrating to the inspector that the house was unfinished. Whatever the reason, *trullis* are also immensely efficient —cool in the summer, warm in winter. You can still visit these unique little houses set amid almond and olive trees while watching local residents create ceramics in a method and style that goes back five hundred years. Lecce is an impressive city and because of its wealth of Baroque architecture, is often referred to as the Florence of the South. Just twenty kilometers north of Gargano lay the gem-like Tremiti Islands, a favorite summer weekend retreat for Italians from the neighboring regions. The

islands are accessible only by a one-hour boat ride from Termoli, or a three-hour ride from Pascara.

Classic Cuisine: The entire region is a massive farmland that generates copious amounts of tomatoes, grapes, melons, oranges, figs, mandarins, lemons, artichokes, lettuce, wild chicory, fennel, peppers, onions, grains, and olive oil. The locals of Puglia are most proud of their pasta, which very often comprises the heart of the meal. Italy's best durum wheat is used to produce the region's most celebrated pasta, *orecchiette* (little ears), along with other cuts that include *maccheroni, spaghetti,* and *cavatelli. Gnocchi* are also popular. A specialty of this area, particularly during Lent, is the *Scalcione di cipolla Puglia,* a *calzone* with onions, black olives, capers, tomatoes, Pecorino cheese, anchovies, and parsley. The sea brims with fish, particularly cuttlefish, oysters, mussels, octopus, and clams. Try a fresh bowl of *zuppa di pesce* (fish chowder) or *cozze ripiene,* stuffed mussels with cheese, herbs, and bread. The main meat in Puglia is lamb, served on a spit, roasted, stewed, as well as fried. Sheep's milk cheese is found in abundance, especially fresh Ricotta,

Pecorino, and the Mozzarella-like Burrata di Andria. Puglia is also notable for its extraordinary, deep green olive oil. Still, grapes are probably the region's most important crop, produced in vast amounts for both eating and wine-making. A meal in Puglia often concludes with a sweet melon, usually watermelon, and grapes.

Classic Wines: Puglia lies along a broad expanse of coastline and is the least mountainous region in Italy. This flat and fertile growing area is mostly dedicated to high-yielding vineyards that produce bulk wine destined for Vermouth and spirit production. There are some producers that specialize in limited production. Primitivo, genetically proven to be a cousin of America's Zinfandel grape, produces some quality examples.

Classic Pairings: Primitivo has the perfect amount of jammy intense fruit. This is a delightful complement to the region's grilled or fried lamb.

Basilicata

The Basilicata is surrounded to the north and east by Puglia and the Ionian Sea, to the south by Calabria, and to the west by the Tyrrhenian Sea and Campania. Before the Romans conquered Basilicata, the region was known as Lucania. Although often overlooked by travelers, its captivating, stark mountain scenery has great vacationing possibilities, especially for bona fide travelers with a zest for adventure. Basilicata contains many places of significant interest. At the lakes of Monticchio, walking, biking, boating, and fishing are enjoyable ways to soak in the surrounding natural environment and panoramic views. The large sandy shorelines along the Ionian coast contain many picturesque seaside resorts that resemble those of the Amalfi coast, yet which remain blissfully free of tourism. Maratea, with its attractive surrounding villages, is one of the loveliest resorts

along this jagged, rocky coastline of the south Tyrrhenian Sea, and is ideal for boating, diving, fishing, swimming, and snorkeling. The ancient Greek ruins at Metaponto and Policoro, archaeological digs, hilltop medieval towns, churches, and Renaissance frescoes are outstanding. A unique experience, and one not to be missed, is a tour of the "Caves of Matera." These shelters dug out of the tufa rock are considered the first houses of the Neolithic inhabitants of the region.

Classic Cuisine: The woodlands and meadows of Basilicata produce bountiful amounts of fruits, vegetables, legumes, cereals, and herbs with splendid fragrances, especially cumin, chives, rosemary, mint, and wild fennel. The sheep and goats fed on these aromatic herbs produce very savory meats that are then grilled, braised, or baked. Here, pigs are held in high esteem and fed almost exclusively on natural foods, such as beans, corn, and acorns. The result is what many people consider the best pork sausage in all of Italy, the *salsicce lucane* or *lucanica*, a tribute to the region's former name. Another specialty of the region is the *peperone di Senise*, or Senise pepper, traditionally used for flavoring peasant dishes and often used for making local cheeses, cured meats, and for flavoring soups. Cheeses produced in this region are outstanding, and the majority are made from sheep's milk. Pecorino Lucano is of the highest quality and is often used as an ingredient in various culinary preparations. The Cacioricotta cheeses, ancient in their

origins, are a timeless blend of goat's and sheep's milk, unifying into a strong and tangy flavor perfect for grating onto pasta dishes. Desserts are also very good, especially those sweetened with local honeys such as *grano dolce* (sweet wheat).

Classic Wines: Basilicata is the third smallest region in Italy in terms of population, and it produces very little wine. However, the Aglianico del Vulture Superiore was granted DOCG status in 2010, and it shows great complexity with age. Wines labeled "Riserva" have been aged a minimum of five years, two of them in wood.

Classic Pairings: The aged Aglianico has enough body to stand up against the popular local delicacy, a pork sausage known as *lucanica*, and it has a cleansing dark fruit finish.

Calabria

Calabria encompasses the tip of Italy's peninsula, bordered by Basilicata to the north, extending down between the Tyrrhenian and the Ionian seas, and is divided from Italy by the Strait of Messina. Its most populous city is Reggio, which sits on the "toe" of the boot and is separated from Sicily by the strait of Messina. The seat of the Calabrian government, Reggio is also known as the City of Bronzes for its famous Riace statues dating from ancient Greece, and for its cultivation of bergamot, a popular perfume ingredient. The inland area is scattered with small, picturesque villages embracing the hills that slope down to meet the water, along with attractive citrus plantations and olive groves. Calabria has extraordinary landscapes encompassing rugged mountains, infinite wheat fields, and dazzling clear seas. Here is a region with one of the most unrestricted coastline beaches in Europe,

making it ideal for boating, swimming, and fishing. Traveling inland towards La Sila Grande, you will come across miles of evergreen forests with snow-capped mountains, streams, and waterfalls. Calabria is home to two national parks: Aspromonte National Park, made up of crystalline granite resembling an enormous pyramid, and Pollino National Park, home to many rare plants and animal species and the largest protected area among the recent parks established in Italy. Calabria is one of the regions that has stayed most true to its heritage. In the small villages, elderly men still spend much time playing cards at tables in the town piazzas, as the older woman, still dressed in traditional black, sit together near their homes to chat about the local news.

Classic Cuisine: Most of the cuisine of Calabria is greatly influenced by the Mediterranean. The foods of the region primarily consist of fresh pastas, vegetables cooked in a variety of ways, and meats, though mainly pork. Eggplant is a favorite vegetable and is creatively prepared in a few variations. *Involtini di melanzane con salsa di pomodoro* are eggplant rollups stuffed with Mozzarella and Parmesan cheese, fresh herbs, and breadcrumbs, then topped with a light tomato sauce. Even with an abundance of fish, the region holds pasta in the highest regard, with each city or town specializing in its own dish. Calabrians pride themselves in creating perfect pasta sauces as well, carefully matching each one to create the tastiest dish possible. The varieties are seemingly endless, running from seafood and meat sauces to those that incorporate tomatoes and a variety of other vegetables. Black pepper and *pepperoncini* are extensively used as seasonings, giving Calabrian food its notoriously spicy flavor. Calabrian cooks also pride themselves on utilizing only the freshest seasonal ingredients possible.

Classic Wines: The vast majority of wine produced in Calabria is red. The most planted grape is Gaglioppo, which is used in the production of reds and *rosatos*. The legend is that this is an ancient variety brought over from Greece, but recent DNA evidence proves it is genetically linked to Sangiovese. Although very little whites are made, the DOC of Melissa produces nice wines from the Greco grape.

Classic Pairings: The whites from Melissa pair nicely with the popular eggplant dishes of the region.

Sicily

Sicily is the largest island in the Mediterranean, and it is considered the most important economically. It is also justly famous for its historical and artistic heritage. The island is encircled by the Tyrrhenian Sea to the north, the Ionian Sea to the east, and the Sicilian Sea to the southwest. The Strait of Messina separates the island from Calabria. Sicily is the most expansive region in Italy. It encompasses the outlying Pelagie Islands, Ustica, Egadi, Pantelleria, and the Aeolian Islands, which consist of Lipari, Salina, Stromboli, Panarea, Vulcano, Alicudi, and Filicudi. On the Aeolian Islands,

you will find stunning panoramas, volcanoes, ancient castles, archaeological museums, a variety of water sports, excellent fishing, and fine beaches. Sicily abounds with many wonderful places of interest: Agrigento is a city of exceptional archaeological heritage; Catania is positioned on the Gulf of Catania and stretches over the southern base slopes of Europe's highest active volcano, Mount Etna; Ragusa is one of the most authentic Sicilian areas, with quintessential towns, magnificent wide sandy beaches, and crystal-clear seas; Syracuse exudes a strong connection with its ancient Greek past, both from a mythological and historical point of view; Palermo is Sicily's largest and most modern city, while Taormina is a captivating medieval town with unrivaled views of Mount Etna and the Ionian coast, along with a truly chic ambience.

Classic Cuisine: The cuisine of Sicily is distinctive from most other Italian regions. The Greeks, Romans, Arabs, Normans, French, and Spanish have all had some bearing on the island's cuisine. There exists an imaginative combination of sweet and sour essences. The generous use of aromatic herbs, exceptional olive oil, abundant fresh seafood, decadent desserts, succulent fruits, olives, almonds, and prickly pears sets Sicilian cooking apart from all others. Sicilians also adore their seafood, prepared in popular dishes such as grilled snapper, *Pesci Spada con Salsa Arancione* (swordfish with orange sauce), and *Tonno con Capperi* (tuna with capers). *Vitello al Marsala* (veal Marsala) is the most popular meat dish, but is only one of the countless meat specialties of the region. Pasta is consumed daily in such famous dishes as *cannelloni* (stuffed pasta with meat, cheese, nutmeg, and pepper), or served with a rich, spicy tomato sauce. Some typical Sicilian antipasti are: *caponata*, a pâté-like mixture of eggplant, olives, capers, and celery served on crusty bread, and *arancini*, which are fried rice balls stuffed with beef, chicken, and cheese. Some other characteristic dishes that incorporate the typical produce of the land are *Spaghetti alla Norma*, prepared with fried eggplants, basil, and Ricotta *Salata* cheese, and *sfinciune*, a *focaccia* served with chopped onions, tomatoes, anchovies, and cheese. Sicilian desserts are outstanding: *cannolis* are cylinder-like pastries stuffed with creamed and sweetened Ricotta cheese; *Cassata alla Siciliana* is the most adored Sicilian cake, usually served at Easter and filled with the identical rich Ricotta filling used in *cannolis*; *cubbaita*, a nougat with honey, almonds, and sesame seeds; and, of course, Sicilian *gelato* (ice cream).

Classic Wines: Sicily is one of Italy's largest wine producers in terms of volume. Despite this output, and its history of great food and olive oil, Sicilian wines have never had a great reputation. Perhaps its best-known is Marsala, a fortified wine that was likely introduced to a broader audience by English explorer John Woodhouse during his 1773 expedition to the island. While fortified wines were popular throughout Europe at the time, today Marsala is mostly regarded as a cooking wine to those who live outside

Italy. For that reason, contemporary winemakers have great difficulty shaking this negative and often unfair reputation. Still, there are some impressive wines coming out of Sicily. Producers such as Marco de Bartoli, Planeta, and Palari are just a few of the vineyards producing great wines. The area to keep your eye on is Mt. Etna. Although it is extremely difficult and dangerous to grow grapes so close to an active volcano, these vineyards are producing some mind-blowing wines. Sicily also boasts a host of native grapes, such as Nero d'Avola, that make nice wines, and the international varietal IGTs are typically of the most consistent quality.

Classic Pairings: Nero d'Avola and Vitello al Marsala is a local favorite. The grape enhances veal dishes without overpowering the flavors.

Sardinia

Situated in the middle of the western Mediterranean just twelve kilometers from Corsica, Sardinia is the second-largest island in Italy. Modern-day Sardinia has become a beloved holiday site for both affluent Italians and travelers from abroad. If your ideal holiday includes countless beautiful sandy beaches, small islands with turquoise seas, and some of Europe's most spectacular scenery, you cannot beat Sardinia's western coast. Starting up north with Costa Smerelda, and working down to the Gulf of Cagliari in the south, this is where you will find some of the island's best sailing, reef diving, waterskiing, scuba diving, wind surfing, fishing, biking, rock climbing, and archaeological ruins. World-class boutiques, cafés, and restaurants fill resort towns like Porto Rotondo and Porto Cervo. The city of Cagliari, Sardinia's capital, is not only home to several first-class resorts, but is also well worth a visit in and of itself. Established by the Phoenicians in the 7th century B.C., it features monuments, architecture, and archaeological wonders from the various cultures that arrived in port and left their mark. Highlights include the city's old harbor district; the hilltop *Castello* (castle) with its spectacular views; the Basilica di San Saturnino, one of the island's most important Palaeo-Christian monuments; and the Sardinian Archaeological Museum. Located on the northwest coast, Alghero is considered one of the loveliest towns in Sardinia, and has preserved the architecture and language of its Catalonian past. La Maddalena Archipelago has a few beaches and many historical sites, including

Garibaldi's final home and resting place on the island of Caprera nearby. In the town of Castelsardo, it is worth visiting the natural sandstone formations of Santa Teresa di Gallura, the ancient towers and fortifications, the Doria Castle, and the 12th-century church of Santa Maria di Tergu. Sardinians are also people of the land, with many still working as shepherds and farmers further inland.

Classic Cuisine: Sardinian cuisine mixes the bounty of both land and sea, centering on bread, pasta, wine, cheese, olive oil, and sweets. Sheep, lamb, pig, and fish are commonly roasted, a preparation that best retains the meat's tenderness while cooking it to perfection. Other specialties include artichokes, wild mushrooms, saffron, and, of course, the prized Pecorino Sardo and Fiore Sardo cheeses, which are produced from sheep and goat and served either fresh or aged. Today, these animals still roam the same pristine terrain§ that they have for centuries, generating the identical mild and delicious flavors of ancient Sardinia. Spicy fish soups called burrida (fish boiled with garlic, fish liver, and chopped walnuts) and cassola de pisci (fish soup richly seasoned with spicy tomato sauce) along with lobsters, crabs, anchovies, squid, clams, and fresh sardines are all very popular along the Sardinian coast. Alghero especially is famous for

lobster, typically prepared by boiling and simply served with olive oil, salt, and a hint of lemon or incorporated into a sauce over pasta. Should you prefer meat, the famous malloreddus (saffron-flavored dumplings) with sausage, tomatoes, sheep or goat cheese, and culingionis (filled ravioli pockets with Ricotta or goat cheese) is a must. Every special feast-day, such as Carnival, Christmas, and Easter, has its own unique desserts. The basic ingredients are typically almonds, oranges, lime peels, cinnamon, vanilla, raisins, walnuts, sugar, and honey. Often Ricotta or freshly grated Pecorino is incorporated.

Classic Wines: The island of Sardinia is known for its Spanish grapes. The most prevalent red grapes are Cannonau, in Spain called Garnacha (Grenache), and Carignano (Cariñena). For whites, Vermentino is the most planted. The island's only DOCG is Vermentino di Gallura. Further inland, Cannonau produces spicy, full-bodied reds. A real treat is the fortified dessert wine Vernaccia di Oristano by the Attilio Contini winery. They have long had a reputation for producing amazing wines, and their Vernaccias are unrivaled.

Classic Pairings: Vermentino is the traditional accompaniment for the spicy fish soup called burrida. It quells the spice and plays upon the delicacy of fresh seafood flavors.

BORGO EGNAZIA

72010 Savelletri di Fasano | Brindisi, Italy

Tel: +39 080225500, ext 850

E-mail: info@borgoegnazia.com

Website: www.borgoegnazia.com / www.sandomenicohotels.com

BORGO EGNAZIA is a world-class property providing extraordinary hospitality and unforgettable holidays. Whether you're seeking a romantic interlude, spa excursion, golf outing, beach retreat, or family getaway, all in a stunning Mediterranean setting, then look no further. Nestled among Apulian olive groves and located just a few minutes from the sparkling shores of the Adriatic, this pristinely elegant property perfectly interprets contemporary ideals of beauty and hospitality. Conceived and developed over a span of ten years under the guidance of artist Pino Brescia, Borgo Egnazia is a visionary interpretation of a typical Apulian village and an homage to indigenous resources, from the locally sourced, hand cut limestone of the buildings to the flowering bougainvillea and jasmine that perfume the enclosed gardens. The layout provides guests with an equal measure of privacy and exclusive access, and includes three kinds of accommodations: La Corte, the main hotel with its 63 rooms and suites; Il Borgo, a separate village that offers one- and two-bedroom townhouses surrounding a central piazza; one seven-room villa; and twenty-eight three-bedroom villas, each featuring private pools, gardens, and wraparound rooftop terraces. The on-site Vair Spa is a sanctuary for the body, mind, and spirit, operating in accordance with a psychoemotional vision that places inner beauty at the core of its spa treatments. Borgo Egnazia's culinary offerings include six restaurants, each with a specific identity related to the tradition of Puglia, from the sophisticated gourmet experience of Due Camini, helmed by Michelin-starred chef Andrea Ribaldone and new executive chef Domingo Schingaro, or lunch at the Beach Club Cala Masciola, with its panoramic sea views and fresh grilled fish. Lobster, shrimp, tuna, sea brim, sea bass, mussels, and octopus—everything comes straight from the sea, set on ice until ready to grill. Sitting at the open-air restaurant is one of those moments you are forced to say, "life is good!"

FINE POINTS

Rooms: 28 3-bedroom villas; 1 7-bedroom villa; 92 rooms and townhouses; 63 rooms and suites in main hotel.

Food: Innovative flavors fused with exquisite regional fare at Due Camini; light meals accompanied by relaxing music at the Pool Bar; lunch at Pescheria da Vito at the beach club Cala Masciola; authentic traditional dishes at La Frasca Restaurant and Trattoria Mia Cucina. Traditional Mediterranean cuisine at Il Cortile buffet; Da Puccetta children's restaurant.

Special Features: One indoor and 3 outdoor swimming pools; 1 grass and 2 synthetic tennis courts; 19,000-square-foot Vair Spa offering a variety of treatments, 10 treatment rooms, couples rooms, spacious wet area with Tepidarium (warm room), Calidarium (hot room), and Frigidarium (cold room), two Roman-bath scrub rooms, customized body and facial treatments, full range of beauty services, a salon and barber shop, and Technogym fitness facility with yoga studio; world-class golfing available next door at renowned San Domenico Golf Course; cooking school; beach club with array of water sports; game room with billiards and board games; kids club and facilities; full-stocked library; bike rentals; nearby sailing, wind and kite surfing, horseback riding, soccer, and kart racing.

COLONNA PEVERO HOTEL

Località Golfo del Pevero | Porto Cervo (OT) | 07021 | Costa Smeralda | Sardinia, Italy

Tel: +39 0789907009 | Fax: +39 078992064

E-mail: info@colonnapeverohotel.it

Website: www.colonnapeverohotel.it

COLONNA PEVERO HOTEL has redefined the Porto Cervo experience through its cuisine, service, and genuine interest in pleasing each and every guest—adults and children alike. It is the perfect place for honeymooners to nestle at the bar overlooking the sea during a spectacular Sardinian sunset, or for families to enjoy together time at one of the hotel's five pools or at the beach. The food is brilliant, whether a candlelit dinner at the established La Terrazza restaurant or experiencing the signature cuisine of Sardinian native and executive chef, Antonio Erriu, at Zafferano, dedicated to those who wish to be seduced by the ultimate gourmet experience in an intimate setting. Chef Erriu's cuisine is, as he states, "constantly evolving, taking its cue both from the traditional recipes of our island and new traits brought from all around the Mediterranean." In keeping with the region's air of relaxed luxury, the Colonna Pevero Hotel offers guests an exceptional resort-style experience, with on-site amenities that include a wellness center offering massage and beauty treatments, a Technogym fitness center, five sparkling pools, access to two private beaches, and golf at the renowned 18-hole, par 72 Golf Club Pevero. Designed by Robert Trent Jones, this championship course has hosted several international events, including the Italian Open in 1978. Since leisure is the name of the game here, the concierge excels at booking a variety of sailing, mountain biking, tennis, horseback riding, diving, deep-sea fishing, and other excursions throughout the area. There is even a nearby polo club. Accommodations include 99 rooms and suites, all outfitted in a mix of modern and traditional furnishings and offering the latest in guest amenities. Most of the rooms have sea views and they all have spacious verandas or terraces.

FINE POINTS

Rooms: 99 rooms and suites. All suites have terraces with sun beds. The executive suite features 1 bedroom and a separate living room; the two-level royal suite has 1 bedroom, large living room, 2 bathrooms, 2 large terraces, 1 outside Jacuzzi; and the luxurious presidential suite features 2 bedrooms, large living room, 3 bathrooms, large terrace, and private pool.

Food: Breakfast and lunch at Le Piscine; prix-fix gourmet dining at La Terrazza; a la carte fine dining at Zafferano; two indoor bars; one pool bar; room service.

Special Features: All rooms feature private bathrooms with bath or shower, direct telephone lines (including in the bathroom), satellite TV, pay-per-view cable TV service, wire radio (including in the bathroom), minibars, lockboxes, free high speed Internet, Wifi, hair dryers, air conditioning, verandas or terraces, and come with free breakfast; five swimming pools; wellness center and Technogym fitness center; conference rooms and business center; private helicopter pad and independent car parks; championship golf course and polo club nearby; concierge can book a variety of sporting and sightseeing excursions.

GARDEN & VILLAS RESORT

Via Provinciale Lacco, 284 | Forio - Isola d'Ischia | 80075 Forio (NA), Italy
Tel: +39 081987311 | Fax: +39 0815071404
E-mail: info@gardenvillasresort.it
Website: www.gardenvillasresort.it

GARDEN & VILLAS RESORT lies just north of Capri on the small island of Ischia, a volcanic outcropping in the Bay of Naples. The terrain is mountainous and scenic, sprinkled with thick forests, vineyards, beaches, picturesque villages, botanical gardens, and historic ruins. The island's volcanic activity has made it famous for the natural spa offerings and thermal gardens, filled with luxurious hot springs and healing volcanic mud. The resort is located walking distance from the sandy beaches of San Montano in seaside Lacco Ameno, arguably the most beautiful commune on the island and home to the Negombo Thermal Gardens, a park full of natural soaking pools and saunas carved from the surrounding rock. Set within two acres of extraordinary gardens, the resort itself blends in perfectly with its diverse landscape, and guests can stroll along flowered stone paths through verdant palms, aromatic herbs, and fragrant fruit trees. The stately guestrooms are part of individual villas nestled in these lovely gardens, each with balconies or terraces, many with sea views, and some with private outdoor Jacuzzis. Set amid the distinctly Mediterranean whitewashed villas and lush vegetation, the outdoor pool is fed by the island's thermic waters and makes for a fabulous spot to enjoy the gorgeous surroundings or a drink at the poolside bar. Additionally, the wellness center has an indoor pool, sauna, and gym, as well as a selection of body treatments and massages that feature local products. The hotel's fare is truly excellent farm-to-table cuisine, highlighting homegrown produce from the on-site organic garden, local seafood, and regional culinary traditions, including fantastic wood-fired breads and Neapolitan pizza. The Il Corbezzolo restaurant has exceptional service, and offers light lunch and romantic dinners, while the terrace bar overlooking the gardens serves snacks and aperitifs. Breakfast here is a highlight, loaded with delicious produce from the gardens as well as freshly baked breads, pastries, fresh preserves, and honey from the island.

FINE POINTS

Rooms: 53 guest rooms.

Food: Breakfast, lunch, and dinner at Il Corbezzolo; room service.

Special Features: Pet friendly; free parking; outdoor pool; wellness center with indoor pool, sauna, massage, body treatments, and gym; Wi-Fi; meeting and banquet facilities, bicycle rental; limousine service.

GRAND HOTEL COCUMELLA

Via Cocumella, 7 | 80065 Sant'Agnello | Sorrento, Italy
Tel: +39 0818782933 | Fax: +39 0818783712
E-mail: info@cocumella.com
Website: www.cocumella.comvv

GRAND HOTEL COCUMELLA boasts a rich and storied history, one that adds an air of romance to this 16th-century property perched high on a cliff on the Amalfi Coast overlooking the Bay of Naples. Located just a short distance to the center of Sorrento, the property was originally built as a Jesuit Monastery amid a splendid park filled with blooming flowers and fragrant orange and lemon trees. Converted into a hotel in 1822, it remains a sought-after spot by travelers seeking the best this part of the country has to offer. The hotel is renowned for mingling Old World elegance with modern amenities—the standard rooms are comfortable and accommodating and the suites downright indulgent, with their jetted tubs, expansive balconies, and outdoor Jacuzzis. At the same time, management prides itself on the skill and warmth of its staff members, all of whom excel at making every guest—including children—feel right at home. The on-site swimming pool, gardens, and beach (accessed via trolley from the hotel) allow for plenty of down time, while those who want to get out and about have only a brisk 10 to 15 minute stroll into the center of Sorrento, resplendent with its own gardens and unique history. Not to be missed is a trip along the Amalfi Coast or a jaunt across the water to Capri on the hotel's very own authentic 1880 tall ship, the Vera. The hotel's Scintilla Restaurant, which overlooks the park, serves beautifully prepared dishes in the Mediterranean tradition along with an assortment of fine Italian wines. Open in the summer, Coku is a Japanese Robata grill/fusion restaurant located on the terrace overlooking the Bay of Naples. Also in summer, guests may enjoy a casual barbecue lunch at L'Agrumeto, which offers outdoor poolside seating under the shade of the orange trees. The on-site cocktail lounge is a lively spot to converse with fellow guests and relax with a perfectly prepared cocktail, beer, or wine.

FINE POINTS

Rooms: 50 total; 7 Full Suites, 7 Junior Suites.

Food: Three on-site restaurants, the Scintilla (open year round), Coku (open mid-June to mid-September), and L'Agrumeto (open in summer); cocktail bar; room service; free breakfast.

Special Features: All rooms are charmingly furnished with antiques, and some feature marble fire places, frescoed ceilings, balconies, and private patios; all rooms include air-conditioning, cable color television, direct dial phone, mini bars, safety deposit boxes, and free Wi-Fi; easy beach access, with private solarium; fitness center and outdoor pool; private chapel for weddings and concerts; business center; tours of the Amalfi Coast, Capri, and nearby towns; small pets allowed free of charge; transfers to and from Naples airport.

HOTEL SIGNUM

Via Scalo, 15 | 98050 Malfa – Salina | Isole Eolie (ME), Italy
Tel: +39 0909844222 | Tel: +39 0909844375 | Fax: +39 0909844102
E-mail: info@hotelsignum.it
Website: www.hotelsignum.it

HOTEL SIGNUM is situated on the verdant island of Salina in the Aeolian Islands, an archipelago located in the Tyrrhenian Sea just north of Sicily. Charming and historic, the hotel is everything discerning travelers seek in a four-star island retreat, owned and operated by husband and wife team Clara Rametta and Michele Caruso. Their passion and dedication has resulted in a gem of a property that represents the ultimate in comfort, relaxation, and beauty. The hotel's thirty delightful rooms are tastefully decorated with native antiques and furnishings. Outside, terraces and balconies provide breathtaking views to the lush gardens and the sea, while the intoxicating scent emanating from the surrounding citrus and jasmine groves perfumes the air. Relaxation is the order of the day, whether at the scenic outdoor infinity pool, inside the elegant library, or at the beach, which is just steps from the hotel. The exclusive on-site Salus per Aquam (SPA) offers guests a host of exceptional skin and body treatments using the islands natural geothermic, mineral-rich waters. A drink at the solarium bar while enjoying views of the neighboring islands of Panarea and Stromboli is the perfect way to continue the day's enchantment into the evening. In the kitchen at Signum Resturant, cooking side-by-side, Chef Michael Caruso and his daughter Chef Martina Caruso create traditional Aeolian dishes with an innovative twist that's nothing short of inspirational. Wine affectionatos will delight in Signum's cellar, which is stocked with carefully selected bottles from all over Italy and Europe, including local rarities with special attention given to small producers, natural and biodynamic wines.

FINE POINTS

Rooms: 30 rooms—classic, superior, and deluxe.

Food: Bar; restaurant serving breakfast, lunch, and dinner; room service.

Special Features: All rooms feature air-conditioning, ceiling fans, satellite television, telephone, Internet access, safety deposit box, and mini bar stocked with Aeolian drinks and snacks; room service; laundry service; on-site SPA with skin and body treatments; outdoor infinity pool; library; hiking trips and scooter and boat tours arranged from hotel.

IL PICCIOLO ETNA GOLF RESORT & SPA

S.S. 120 km, 200 - 95012 | Castiglione di Sicilia (Catania), Italy

Tel: +39 0942986384

E-mail: info@ilpiccioloetnagolfresort.com

Website: www.ilpiccioloetnagolfresort.com

IL PICCIOLO ETNA GOLF RESORT & SPA sits at the foot of Mt. Etna, in an area renowned for its natural beauty and outdoor adventure opportunities. Etna alone provides a variety of prospects, from scenic cable car rides to guided climbs up to the crater of this roughly 10,900-foot peak. Nearby, the Alcantara River cuts through lava flows from Mt. Etna, creating a spectacular gorge where sightseers can wade through cool waters between vertical basalt walls. The area also offers a variety of excellent cycling opportunities, for both road and mountain bikers and single-track lovers or less experienced cyclists. From trail running to volcano skiing, rafting to canyoneering, this spectacular area has no shortage of activities for the adventurous traveler. The Il Picciolo Resort has its own beautiful 18-hole golf course, complete with excellent views of Mt. Etna, instruction from Scottish golf pro Norman Johnston, and an elegant clubhouse with Il Palmento restaurant, which serves lunch from 12:30 p.m to 5:00 p.m. The hotel itself is set amid the beautiful green landscape of Mt. Etna's foothills, flanked by the vineyards of the Etna DOC. The rooms and suites emphasize comfort and relaxation, and feature rustic-chic décor, spacious bathrooms, modern amenities, and panoramic views. The outdoor pool is a wonderful place to take in the views and relax outside, while the spa has an extensive menu of treatments and massage, as well as a sauna, Turkish bath, relaxation area, herbal tea and juice bar, hydrotherapy pool, and fitness center. After a day on the golf course or exploring the area, the La Ghiandaia restaurant serves a hearty meal of Sicilian cuisine with an international twist, accompanied by exclusive local wines.

FINE POINTS

Rooms: 98 rooms.

Food: Breakfast and dinner served at La Ghiandaia; light lunch and snacks available at Il Palmento at the golf course clubhouse; drinks and snacks served at the Birdie Lounge Bar; room service.

Special Features: 18-hole golf course; wellness center and spa with gym facilities, sauna, Turkish bath, whirlpool, hydrotherapy pool, and herbal tea and juice bar; business center with meeting rooms and conference facilities; banquet room; dry cleaning and self-serve laundry; babysitting; Wi-Fi; complimentary parking.

PRAIA ART RESORT

Loc. Praialonga, 88900 | Crotone KR, Italy
Tel: +39 09621902890
E-mail: info@praiaartresort.com
Website: www.praiaartresort.com

PRAIA ART RESORT is tucked away at the edge of the Capo Rizzuto marine reserve along the Ionian coast in Calabria. The perfect getaway for those who want to experience the personalized service of a luxury resort but without the tourist trappings, it casts its spell almost immediately. Located just minutes from the beach, Praia Art Resort offers guests the unique opportunity to explore not only the bays, inlets, and headlands that make up the surrounding coastal environment but also the nearby mountains, quaint villages, ancient castles, and Grecian ruins. The staff excels at creating an experience that is welcoming but discreet, attentive but never intrusive. Even the small resort spa is personalized, set in an environment designed to accommodate the needs of one guest at a time with massage and body treatments that address everything from tight muscles to cellulite to lymph drainage. Clearly, the resort is designed to be your home away from home in whatever way you chose, whether that is to spend the day swaying in a beachside hammock with a book, lounging with a drink by the pool, or engaging your fellow guests in a lively chat about your travels. Each of the fifteen rooms has been individually styled with furnishings, accessories, and artwork crafted from wood, terracotta, and wrought iron, all masterfully rendered by local artisans. Patios and balconies, as well as free Wi-Fi, flat-screen televisions, and mini-bars, are also standard. Upgraded rooms have sea views or direct access to the pool, and the suites feature whirlpool baths and Nespresso machines. The culinary offerings at Pietramare restaurant are likewise designed to ensure that guests experience the best of local and international cuisine in an intimate and immersive environment. Seasonal ingredients brought together with flair and imagination result in meals that are nothing short of a delight to all the senses, beautifully plated and perfectly delicious.

FINE POINTS

Rooms: 15 rooms.

Food: Complimentary breakfast; enjoy lunch, dinner and cocktails at Pietramare restaurant and bar; room service available.

Special Features: Small resort spa offering various massage and body treatments; outdoor pool with terrace and hydromassage corner; beach access with hammocks and free sun loungers and umbrellas; free Wi-Fi throughout hotel; welcome gift of fruit, sweets, and bottle of wine; laundry service; free parking; shuttle bus service to and from Le Castella; multilingual staff.

PUNTA TRAGARA

Via Tragara, 57 | 80073 Capri (NA), Italy
Tel: +39 0818370844 | Fax: +39 0818377790
E-mail: info@hoteltragara.it
Website: www.hoteltragara.com

PUNTA TRAGARA offers guests all the beauty for which the island of Capri is famous, but in a secluded setting far away from the summer crowds. This magnificent island, beloved of everyone from ancient Roman emperors to modern-day movies stars, is no doubt one of the world's most magical vacation destinations. Built in 1920 as the villa for Lombardy-born engineer Emilio Errico Vismara and designed by Le Corbusier, Punta Tragara perches high above the sea like an architectural extension of the surrounding cliffs. In 1968 Count Goffredo Manfredi bought the villa as a holiday home and turned it into a hotel in 1973. Hotel Punta Tragara has enjoyed extraordinary growth ever since, reaching the pinnacle of five-star luxury hospitality on Capri. The count's grandson Goffredo Manfredi continues his family's legacy of world-class service and amenities, laudable culinary offerings, and chic accommodations. None of the rooms or suites are alike. Instead they blend modern and classical elements for a delightfully eclectic effect. All offer spectacular garden or sea views, including of the famous Faraglioni rock formations. Although the hotel is a short walk or scooter ride (rentals available at the hotel) to La Piazzetta, the small square that serves as the center of community life in Capri, there is plenty to engage the body, mind, and spirit on-site as well. Indulge in any number of body and beautifying treatments at Unica Spa, take a stroll along the beach, lounge by the pool, work out at the gym, or check with the concierge to book water and sightseeing excursions—you can even book a trip on a private yacht. Restaurant Monzù and La Pergola lounge will meet all your culinary and libation needs, from hand-mixed house cocktails to the freshest seafood prepared from that day's catch—all of which may be enjoyed along with spectacular sunsets out on the panoramic veranda. The hotel also has a relationship with Mammà, a restaurant overseen by two-star chef Gennaro Esposito that is located just off La Piazzetta.

FINE POINTS

Rooms: 44 rooms, including 6 suites.

Food: Breakfast, lunch, and dinner at on-site Monzù restaurant and offsite Mammà; beer, wine, and cocktails at La Pergola bar.

Special Features: Full-service spa; two outdoor swimming pools; hot tub; fitness center with gym/workout room; two beach clubs below hotel; free Wi-Fi throughout property; dry cleaning, laundry service, and self-serve laundry; concierge; multilingual staff; babysitting; book a private yacht, chauffeur-driven car, helicopter, or scooter right from hotel; free transfers to and from hotel via hydrofoil; 10-minute scenic walk to town.

SAN DOMENICO PALACE HOTEL

Piazza San Domenico, 5 | 98039 Taormina Sicily, Italy

Tel: +39 0942613111

E-mail: res.sandomenico@amthotels.it

Website: www.san-domenico-palace.com

SAN DOMENICO PALACE HOTEL resides inside a former fourteenth-century Dominican monastery located in the heart of the charming town of Taormina, home to Italy's premier summer film festival. Taormina's fame as a vacation destination goes back to the Byzantine era, and the people who have sought respite here over just the past one hundred years is a Who's Who of international artists, writers, and political leaders. For many, San Domenico Palace Hotel was their hotel of choice, and they left glowing dedications inside the pages of the hotel's famed Golden Book. Taormina remains the place in Sicily to see and be seen, and San Domenico Palace Hotel continues its long-standing tradition of five-star service. While the friars' soft steps and psalmodies no longer echo through the corridors, the hotel's management and staff retain their own form of devotion—to court an atmosphere of enchantment and refinement while ensuring every guest's stay is a memorable one. The rooms, many with views of the sea, are luxuriously appointed, and the suites epitomize luxury. One even comes with its own swimming pool. The hotel also boasts manicured gardens resplendent with blooming flowers; a beautiful outdoor swimming pool; the Beauty Stop wellness corner; a full-service fitness area; and the elegant bar and lounge, Oratorio dei Frati. The monastery's former *scripta scriptorum* is now The Boutique, which sells exclusive fashions, precious ceramics, and delicious Sicilian wines and foodstuffs. Further gastronomic adventures are available at the hotel's four restaurants: Il Giardino dei Limoni, an informal luncheon spot located by the pool and open from April through October; Les Bougainvillees, an outdoor terrace eatery; Antico Refettorio, which showcases locally-grown products; and the gourmet Principe Cerami, proud bearer of two Michelin stars, thanks to the culinary artistry of chef Massimo Mantarro.

FINE POINTS

Rooms: 90 rooms and 15 suites.

Food: Poolside bar; Oratorio dei Frati bar; Il Giardino dei Limoni, Les Bougainvilles, Antico Refettorio, Principe Cerami restaurants; room service. Note that children over 6 years old are welcomed at Principe Cerami (pushchair and highchairs are not allowed), while children of all ages are welcome any time at all other restaurants. The concierge, upon request, can provide a baby sitter.

Special Features: Meeting facilities to accommodate events and ceremonies for up to 400 people; Wi-Fi access in all rooms on a complimentary basis; business Internet connection available for a daily charge; the Beauty Stop wellness corner with massages and personalized treatments; fitness center; manicured gardens; outdoor swimming pool that is heated in April, May, and October; babysitting upon request; shuttle to and from the airport for a fee.

SANTAVENERE HOTEL

Via Conte Stefano Rivetti 1 | 85046 Maratea PZ | Italy
Tel: + 39 0973876910 | Fax: + 39 0973877654
E-mail: info@santavenere.net
Website: www.santavenere.it

SANTAVENERE HOTEL, with its stately Beaux Arts design, elegant grounds, and prime beachside location, is a five-star luxury experience with all the advantages of its Amalfi coast neighbor to the north, but without the teeming crowds. Instead, its position against a lush forested hillside just off the Basilicata shore overlooking the Mediterranean ensures a tranquil sojourn amid breathtaking natural beauty. Your options for relaxation and adventure are nearly limitless: enjoy a day of reading by the pool, book a snorkeling or boating trip, hike nearby trails, or lazily wander Maratea harbor, with its quaint shops and restaurants. While reserving a sun lounger and umbrella is often difficult at busy beachside resorts, they are in plentiful supply here, ensuring all guests equal time soaking in the sun and gazing at the turquoise-colored waters at the resort's private beach. Indulge yourself further with a treatment or two at the on-site Le Grotte spa and you'll come away from your facial, mud bath, sauna, or massage feeling extra relaxed and rejuvenated. In keeping with the hotel's period charm, many of the 34 rooms feature authentic 18th- and 19th-century furnishings. Others are decidedly modern. All feature air-conditioning and free Wi-Fi, fine linens, comfortable beds, en-suite bathrooms, and terraces or balconies with lawn or sea views—some also give you a glimpse of the Christ the Redeemer statue that graces a nearby hill. One of the great joys of vacation is an indulgent breakfast spread, and Santavenere doesn't disappoint. This buffet of sweet and savory hot and cold items is complimentary and also lavish, and includes a variety of juices, teas, and coffees. The hotel's summer restaurant, Le Lanterne, with outdoor seating overlooking the sea, excels in exquisite dinner dishes featuring freshly caught seafood. Le Lanterne is open for lunch and dinner in the winter (indoors, and also with a sea view). You may also request your meals be served beachside, by the pool, or in your room.

Rooms: 34 rooms.

Food: Complimentary breakfast; lunch in summer at the Gli Ulivi restaurant by the pool and at Il Carrubo restaurant by the beach; dinner in summer at Le Lanterne restaurant outdoors on the terrace, and for lunch and dinner indoors in winter; cocktails, beer, and wine available during the summer at the Gli Ulivi swimming pool bar and at the Il Carrubo bar, and during the winter at Bar della Casa; coffee bar/café; snack bar; 24-hour room service.

Special Features: Non-smoking rooms on request; seasonal outdoor pool; spa and fitness center offering variety of body and beauty treatments, Turkish bath/hammam, indoor sea-water pool with hydro-massage area, and sauna; gym and workout room; beauty treatment rooms; coiffeur service; private beach; tennis and football court; boat tours; free Wi-Fi throughout property; dry cleaning and laundry service; children's activities; babysitting; shuttle bus service; variety of cultural and sporting activities (hiking, rafting, diving, snorkeling, paragliding) booked from hotel; transfers via land, sea, and private plane; heliport; private boat available for special dinners and excursions; concierge; 24-hour front desk; free on-site parking.

FINE POINTS

THERASIA RESORT SEA & SPA

Località Vulcanello - Isola di Vulcano - 98050 | Lipari (Me), Italy
Tel: +39 0909852555 | Fax: +39 0909852154
E-mail: pierpaolo@therasiaresort.it
Website: www.therasiaresort.it

THERASIA RESORT SEA & SPA is located on the island of Vulcano, the southernmost of the seven Aeolian Islands that comprise a volcanic archipelago in the Tyrrhenian Sea north of Sicily. Only eight square miles in size, Vulcano is a jewel of rare beauty and unspoiled nature, defined by lush vegetation, smoky fumaroles, natural mud pools, and sulfurous warm waters. The volcano dominates the island, and hikers who make the 50-minute trek up its side are rewarded with breathtaking views over the other six islands. Dazzling in its white-stuccoed façade, the hotel is constructed from all-natural native materials, including molten rock from Mount Etna, Sicilian terracotta, and cedar and olive woods—these materials are used to decorate the ninety-seven Mediterranean-style guest rooms as well. Outdoors, a variety of local flora, including cactus, have been integrated beautifully into the landscape and gardens, while two infinity pools bridge the gap between land and sea, making for the perfect spot from which to experience unforgettable sunsets. Both the spacious surrounding terraces and the private beach below are dotted with umbrellas and sun beds for optimal relaxation. Also on site is a top-notch spa and wellness center offering a wide range of beauty and rejuvenating treatments, including hydrotherapy, relaxing baths, and massages using advanced techniques along with aromatherapy and perfumed oils to relieve tiredness and stress. The spa also features an indoor warm water pool and hydro-massage, sauna, Turkish bath, and Emotion shower. The cuisine is locally sourced—fish and seafood from the Aeolian Islands, vegetables from nearby Catania, cheeses from Syracuse, and meat from Nebrodi—and available at three on-site restaurants: I Russuri poor bar, open during the summer months; L'Arcipelago, open during the summer months for breakfast and dinner; and the one-Michelin-starred Il Cappero, which presents creative interpretations of traditional Sicilian cuisine accompanied by carefully selected local and international wines from the hotel's own cellar. Breathtaking views, a candle-lit romantic atmosphere, and exemplary service complete the memorable experience.

FINE POINTS

Rooms: 90 rooms.
Food: Complimentary breakfast; I Russuri pool bar; breakfast and dinner seasonally at L'Arcipelago; dinner year round at Il Cappero.
Special Features: Spa and wellness center with variety of beautifying and rejuvenating treatments; fitness center with gym and workout room; two infinity pools; tennis courts; business center and meeting rooms; wedding services; free Wi-Fi throughout property; concierge; money exchange; doctor on call; laundry service; valet parking.

VERDURA RESORT

S.S. 115 Km 131 | 92019 Sicily, Italy
Tel: +39 0925998001
E-mail: reservations.verdura@roccofortehotels.com
Website: www.roccofortehotels.com/verdura-resort

VERDURA RESORT, a Rocco Forte hotel, is situated on over 550 scenic acres along a mile of pristine private Mediterranean coastline. Redefining the words "luxury resort," Verdura surprises with its spacious yet private ambiance, while also offering the service and amenities that transform a mere vacation into the getaway of a lifetime. Created by renowned interior designer Olga Polizzi, Director of Design for all Rocco Forte hotels, and the Italian architect Flavio Albanese, each of the 153 rooms and 50 suites feature the best in intelligent design and comfort, with private terraces or balconies with seating and sea views, spacious bathrooms, chic furnishings, and luxury bedding and towels. All suites have sea views, and seamlessly meld indoor and outdoor spaces. Two ambassador and one presidential suite feature separate living, kitchen, dining, and sleeping areas, as well as interior courtyards and outdoor terraces that open to expansive views. Verdura Resort is certainly the perfect spot to get away from it all, with its world-class Rocco Forte Spa, beauty and fitness centers, indoor and outdoor pools, three Kyle Phillips's-designed golf courses, six clay tennis courts, and opportunities for water sports and excursions of all kinds. It is also a top spot for traveling gourmands wishing to indulge their passion for exquisitely prepared local specialties. The resort's four restaurants and five bars, all overseen by rising culinary star Fulvio Pierangelini, blend elegant ambiance and stunning views with the best in local, regional, and international cuisine prepared from the freshest ingredients, many of them caught fresh that day or raised on-site at the resort's extensive gardens and lemon and olive orchards. A variety of chef-led cooking, mixology, and wine-tasting classes are a must to augment your experience— whether you wish to learn how to match a wine to your favorite dish, or whip up a specialty pasta, pastry, or cocktail.

FINE POINTS

Rooms: 153 rooms, 47 suites, 2 ambassador suites, and 1 presidential suite.

Food: Four restaurants, five bars, and room service.

Special Features: Three Kyle Phillips golf courses; infinity pool; tennis courts; world-class Rocco Forte Spa, featuring extensive therapeutic treatments, indoor swimming pool, 4 outdoor thalassotherapy pools, steam room, Finnish and infrared saunas, gym and fitness studio, hair and beauty salon, and Spa Bar; indoor and outdoor pools and beach access; complimentary internet service; dry cleaning; full service concierge; multi-lingual staff; business center, conference facilities, and banquet center; children's activities, including a brand-new Kid's Club; babysitting; shuttle bus to and from airport.

"Italy is a dream that keeps returning
for the rest of your life."
— Anna Akhmatova

Photo Credits

Previous Page – Bellevue Hotel & Spa is located in Valle d'Aosta, one of the most splendid and picturesque regions of Italy, bordering both Switzerland and France. The hotel/spa is surrounded by breathtaking views of the Prateria dell'Orso and is opposite a glacier in the heart of the Gran Paradiso National Park in the center of Cogne.

Above – The on-site spa and wellness center of Tuscany's Castel Monastero boasts a broad range of state-of-the-art detoxification, rebalancing, and reshaping therapies.

Back Cover – Top Left: Publishers Drs. David & Debra Levinson, otherwise known as Mr. & Mrs. Italy, enjoying a rapturous moment on the stunning beach of Punta Bianca Agrigento, Sicily. Top Right: open-air massages at Lefay Resort & Spa Lago di Garda dissolves tensions and delivers a deep feeling of relaxation. Bottom Left: Romantik Hotel Turm's restaurant has been voted one of the five best hotel restaurants in Italy, and makes for a wonderful romantic dinner, either inside the cozy dining room or outside on the terrace, surrounded by the magnificence of Mother Nature. Chef Stefan's signature style is both inventive and down-to-earth, and his dishes pair beautifully with any number of wines from the hotel's cellars. Bottom right: Minutes from Lake Garda, Villa Cordevigo Wine Relais is home to *Michelin* one-star restaurant Oseleta, whose executive chef, Giuseppe D'Aquino, orchestrates various culinary elements into a symphonic whole. Dinner is the best time to sample not only various regional dishes but also its wines, including those made on the premises from Bardolino Classico and Cavaion Veronese grapes.